# FRED GRANT AT VICKSBURG

## A BOY'S MEMOIR AT HIS FATHER'S SIDE DURING THE AMERICAN CIVIL WAR

Edited and annotated by

ALBERT A. NOFI

Savas Beatie
California

First edition, first printing

ISBN-13: 978-1-61121-741-4 (paperback)
ISBN-13: 978-1-954547-68-1 (ebook)

Library of Congress Cataloging-in-Publication Data

Names: Grant, Frederick Dent, 1850-1912 author | Nofi, Albert A. editor
Title: Fred Grant at Vicksburg : A Boy's Memoir at His Father's Side During
   the American Civil War / [edited] by Albert A Nofi.
Description: El Dorado Hills, CA : Savas Beatie, 2025. | Includes
   bibliographical references and index. | Summary: "On March 29, 1863,
   12-year-old Frederick Grant, the eldest son of Union Maj. Gen. Ulysses
   S. Grant, arrived at his father's headquarters at Young's Point,
   Louisiana. Grant's Army of the Tennessee was preparing to move against
   Vicksburg, Mississippi, and young Fred had no intention of missing out
   on the adventure. For nearly 100 days, young Fred roamed freely within
   the army, often not seeing his father for days while living amongst the
   troops, sharing their rations, and seeing war firsthand. This is one of
   the greatest yet least-known adventure stories of the age. This
   entertaining and enlightening new study adds another facet to our
   understanding of Vicksburg, the Civil War, and the unique relationship
   of father and son"-- Provided by publisher.
Identifiers: LCCN 2024060961 | ISBN 9781611217414 paperback | ISBN
   9781954547681 ebook
Subjects: LCSH: Vicksburg (Miss.)--History--Siege, 1863--Personal
   narratives | Grant, Ulysses S. (Ulysses Simpson), 1822-1885 | Grant,
   Frederick Dent, 1850-1912
Classification: LCC E475.27 .G793 2025 | DDC 973.7/82--dc23/eng/20250313
LC record available at https://lccn.loc.gov/2024060961

SB
Savas Beatie
989 Governor Drive, Suite 101
El Dorado Hills, CA 95762
916-941-6896 / sales@savasbeatie.com / www.savasbeatie.com

All of our titles are available at special discount rates for bulk purchases in the United States. Contact us for information.

Mary Griner Spencer Nofi,

Marilyn J. Spencer,

Lorie Fawcett, and

Matilda Virgilio Clark

Frederick D. Grant at about 15, in 1865, wearing a school uniform.
*Wisconsin Historical Society*

# TABLE OF CONTENTS

# LIST OF MAPS

# List of Illustrations

# LIST OF ILLUSTRATIONS
## (CONTINUED)

# Preface

# My Encounter with Fred Grant

> My son accompanied me through the campaign and siege and caused no
> anxiety either to me or to his mother, who was at home. He looked out for
> himself and was in every battle of the campaign. His age, then not quite
> thirteen, enabled him to take in all he saw, and to retain a recollection of it
> that would not be possible in more mature years.
>
> —Ulysses S. Grant, *Personal Memoirs*[1]

Having been doing Civil War history for some time, I had occasionally encountered mention of the fact that young Frederick Dent Grant had accompanied his father on campaign at times during the war. I thought it just a curious factoid, that perhaps the lad had served as his father's orderly, or merely was there to keep him company. Then a recent book on the Vicksburg campaign recounted one of Fred's escapades, which piqued my interest, and reminded me that Fred's name had appeared in other works on the campaign. Checking the reference, I hunted down the source, a speech Fred made in 1907 at the annual reunion of the Society of the Army of the Tennessee.[2] What I discovered was five thousand words about the experiences of a 12-year-old hanging out with the Army of the Tennessee for over three months during the campaign for and siege of Vicksburg, and a real adventure story far superior even to Kipling's fictional Kim O'Hara's.[3]

Digging further, it turned out that the speech was Fred's standard address when invited to reunions and other events, one which he had given over the years, each version usually a little different from earlier ones, all of which were often circulated in print. Then I found that at the request of the editor of the *National Tribune*, a veterans' weekly newspaper, Fred had written a much longer memoir, some 18,000 words, which had been serialized in January and February of 1887. This memoir told of his adventures in the field in far more detail, with many

---

1 Ulysses S. Grant, *Personal Memoirs of U. S. Grant* (New York, 1885), I:487.

2 For references to this speech and its variants, and Fred Grant's other writings, see the bibliography.

3 For Kim O'Hara, see *Kim*, by Rudyard Kipling.

more anecdotes and observations on the campaign, his father, and many others, accompanied by some fanciful engravings.[4]

Of course, there were quite a number of boys of Fred's age (and even younger) in the army, as field musicians and occasionally as combatants who'd lied about their age, some of whom attained a measure of fame.[5] But those drummer boys—and occasional drummer girl disguised as a boy—and the underage soldiers in the ranks, were part of the army, and thus lived, worked, and moved under discipline within their regiments. In contrast, Fred roamed where he would, hung out with the troops, went off on little adventures, picked up souvenirs, slept where he could, evaded capture, hobnobbed with generals, witnessed battles, scrounged for food, and was at times under fire, being wounded once, and often did not see his father for days on end.

His was an experience a lot freer than any modern notion of a "free range" childhood, which seemed to this writer to be a story worthy of being made available to a wider audience, which led to this book.[6]

Over the years Fred Grant delivered several short accounts of his wartime adventures in speeches, which were often published. In addition, he occasionally recounted some of his adventures in interviews that appeared in newspapers or other publications. Over a dozen versions of his memoirs are listed in the bibliography, but there may be others that were not found in time to be included here. In all of the versions there is usually some variation among the details of events, and some things can be found in one version that are not in any of the others.

The longest of Fred's reminiscences, the 18,000 words that appeared in the *National Tribune* in January and February of 1887, comprise the text that is reproduced below. Where one of the other versions varies from this version, the difference will be accounted for in footnotes.

Fred noted that he wrote these memoirs almost entirely from memory, not resorting to any references or documents. For a time during the Vicksburg

4  On the *National Tribune*, see Appendix V.

5  For example, drummer Orion Pegasus Howe of the Company C, 55th Illinois Infantry, mentioned below on page 51, put in a Medal of Honor performance when he was 14, and William J. Johnston, a drummer in Company D, 3rd Vermont Infantry, did so at 12.

6  "Free range child raising" is defined as allowing children "of sufficient age and maturity to avoid harm or unreasonable risk of harm, to engage in independent activities." Supposedly this is how many of us grew up before the age of "helicopter moms," "over-scheduled" childhoods, and before cell phones and GPS tracking of cell phones, though from experience I can say that we were often rather lacking in the "sufficient . . . maturity" department; Donna De La Cruz, "Utah Passes 'Free-Range' Parenting Law," *New York Times*, March 29, 2018.

campaign, he kept a journal, though we do not know for how long or how faithfully, or if he had access to it in later years. It seems to have been lost.[7]

Since he was writing from memory, Fred at times got a name or a place wrong, and in at least one instance conflated two important events into one, a matter explained in the footnotes. Footnotes also provide extra details or observations about some of Fred's adventures. He was also careless about dates, and where it seems necessary these are indicated within brackets. Details about persons and places mentioned in the text are found in the appendices.

Spelling, grammar, capitalization, punctuation, and usage in Fred's text are as found in the originals, reflecting contemporary practice and his personal idiosyncrasies. When quoting letters and documents, errors and even cross-outs have been left standing. A [sic] is sometimes used to indicate these.

Being a mid-nineteenth century white American, Fred's account includes some phrases about African Americans that would today be considered offensive, though in his times would not have been so thought, given contemporary usage.

Throughout this work "Grant" refers to the general.

---

7  Grant to Julia, June 9, 1863, "He has kept a journal which I have never read but suppose he will read to you." Ulysses S. Grant, *The Papers of Ulysses S. Grant*, eds. John Y. Simon, et al. (Carbondale, IL, 1969–2012), vol. 8, 33, hereafter cited as Grant, *Papers*.

# SECTION I

# THE MEMOIR

## GENERAL ULYSSES S. GRANT: HIS SON'S
## MEMORIES OF HIM IN THE FIELD

### Fred Grant on the Opening of the Vicksburg Campaign

On November 7, 1907, Fred Grant delivered the opening address at the 37th reunion of the Society of the Army of the Tennessee, at Vicksburg. He began with an overview of the campaign, and this portion of his address on that occasion, describing events before he arrived at the front, reviews the military background to the final phase of the Vicksburg campaign, setting the stage for his adventures with the army through to the surrender of Vicksburg.[1]

Mr. President, comrades of the Army of the Tennessee, ladies and gentlemen:

I feel deeply gratified in the honor of being invited to meet you here this evening, and in being asked to speak to you on this occasion, though my natural modesty convinces me that there are others present, who should take my place on this platform; and well knowing my imperfections, I wish for your sake that a more finished orator had been chosen. I hesitated much as to the subject which might prove most interesting, when I accepted the complimentary invitation to address you tonight.

This being the reunion of the Army of the Tennessee, and that reunion in the city of Vicksburg, I feel it may be appropriate for me to speak of the campaign and siege of Vicksburg as taken from official records, as well as of incidents seen by me when a boy of twelve years of age, accompanying his soldier father through that terrible but glorious and heroic epoch of our National history.

---

1  Frederick D. Grant, "Annual Address," *Report of the Proceedings of the Society of the Army of the Tennessee at the Thirty-Seventh Meeting, Held at Vicksburg, Mississippi, November 7–8, 1907* (Cincinnati, 1908), 95–99.

Maj. Gen. Henry Halleck,
Commanding General of the Army
*Library of Congress*

Soon after the battle of Corinth, Mississippi, which occurred on October 4th, 1862, General Grant suggested to the General-in-Chief, Halleck, a forward movement against the Confederate forces at Vicksburg.[2]

On October 25th, General Grant was placed in command of the Union forces of the Department of the Tennessee, and securing some additional troops from the North, he was on November 2d prepared to take the initiative.

Vicksburg was of very great importance to the North, because when that city and its environments were held by the Confederates, free navigation of the Mississippi River was interfered with, and the products of the Northwest could not be cheaply transported to the sea. Vicksburg was of greater importance to the South, as from that city a railroad running east led to all points in the Southern States, and on the opposite side of the Mississippi River there was another railroad extending westward. Vicksburg was the channel of communication for the Confederates on the east and west of the Mississippi, and it was of great military strength, occupying as it did the first high ground near the river below Memphis. Points on the Mississippi River between Vicksburg and Port Hudson were held as dependencies by the Confederates and were sure to fall upon the capture of Vicksburg.

At that time the Army of the Tennessee had possession of the Mobile & Ohio Railroad from about twenty-five miles south of Corinth, north to Columbus, Kentucky and the Mississippi Central Railroad from Bolivar, Tennessee, north to its junction with the Mobile & Ohio Railroad. This army also held the Memphis & Charleston Railroad from Corinth, east to Bear Creek, as well as the shore of the Mississippi River from Cairo, Illinois, to Memphis, Tennessee.

---

2  For persons mentioned in the text, see Appendix I; For places named in the text, see Appendix II.

(Left) Maj. Gen. Ulysses S. Grant, called "Old Man" by his troops. (Right) Lt. Gen. John C. Pemberton, Commander of the Confederate Army of the Mississippi. *Library of Congress*

The moving force of the Army of the Tennessee was about 30,000 men, and it was estimated the confronting force, commanded by the Confederate General Pemberton, consisted of about the same number of soldiers. The Union right wing was commanded by General Sherman, who was located at Memphis, the center by General Hurlburt, and the left wing by General McPherson. General Pemberton was fortified at the Tallahatchie River with a force thrown forward to Holly Springs and Grand Junction on the Mississippi Central Railroad.

The forward movement of the Union forces under General Grant's command commenced on November 2d, 1862, and on November 4th Grand Junction and La Grange were occupied by General McPherson's command and the troops were pushed out some seven or eight miles further south, along the line of the railroad, which latter was repaired as the troops advanced. On the 13th the cavalry in advance reached Holly Springs and the Confederates fell back south of the Tallahatchie River.

Holly Springs was selected for the Union Army's depot of supplies, and munitions of war were collected there. Sherman at Memphis was ordered forward and reached on the 29th Cottage Hill, ten miles north of Oxford. The Union troops at Helena, Arkansas, west of the Mississippi, were directed to cross the river and cut the railroad in rear of Pemberton's forces. This last movement, under Generals Hovey and Washburn, was successful so far as reaching the railroad was concerned, but the damage done by the troops was slight and soon repaired by the Confederates.

The Tallahatchie River was high, the bridges destroyed, and the Confederate forces strongly fortified on the south side of the river, so a crossing in their front was impossible. The Union cavalry were sent up the river to find a ford and were successful. This, in conjunction with the expedition from Helena, caused Pemberton to evacuate his fortified position on the Tallahatchie and go south. He was followed by the main body of the Union troops as far as Oxford and by McPherson's command for about seventeen miles further. Here the pursuit was halted, for repairing the railroad to the rear. On the 8th of December General Sherman was ordered back to Memphis to take command of an expedition down the Mississippi River for an attack on Vicksburg.

On December 20th, when all seemed progressing favorably toward the capture of Vicksburg, the Confederate General Van Dorn appeared before Holly Springs, the Union base of supplies, captured the garrison of 1,500 men and destroyed all the munitions of war, food and forage there. The surrender of Holly Springs demonstrated the impossibility of maintaining the long line of railroad to Columbus, over which to draw supplies, and the campaign as at first planned was abandoned and General Grant decided to so change the plan as to make the Mississippi River the line over which to transport supplies to the Union forces operating against Vicksburg.

While the surrender of Holly Springs was disgraceful, it nevertheless proved of great value to the Union forces, for being thus without supplies they were obliged to live off of the country, and finding how easily this could be done, the greatest difficulty of the problem of the campaign by which Vicksburg was captured was solved, as was the question of supplying Sherman's army in its campaign from Atlanta to the sea.

The expedition down the Mississippi under General Sherman to attack Vicksburg was unsuccessful; he attacked the Confederates located upon Walnut Hills and failed to carry the hills, retired to his transports and returned to the mouth of the Arkansas River, where he learned of a Confederate garrison at Arkansas Post, some fifty miles up the Arkansas River. He turned his forces against this garrison and after a sharp fight, being assisted by the gunboats under Admiral Porter, he captured it with 5,000 prisoners and seventeen cannon and then returned to the town of Napoleon on the Mississippi River.

New plans for the capture of Vicksburg having been made, the Northern army, which had been somewhat increased by reinforcements, was divided into four corps, the Thirteenth, Fifteenth, Sixteenth and Seventeenth, commanded respectively by Generals McClernand, Sherman, Hurlburt and McPherson. Three corps, the Thirteenth, Fifteenth and Seventeenth, were moved down the Mississippi as near as possible to Vicksburg and placed on the west bank of the river. Owing to the high water they could camp only on the levee and the three

(Left) Rear Adm. David Dixon Porter. *The Photographic History of the Civil War*
(Right) Maj. Gen. William T. Sherman, photographed by Mathew Brady in 1864. *Library of Congress*

corps occupied the river front from Young's Point through Milliken's Bend to Lake Providence, seventy miles above Vicksburg. Hurlburt, with the Sixteenth Corps, was left to guard the rear and occupy the territory of value to the Union forces in Northern Mississippi and Western Tennessee.

By the end of January 1863, General Grant arrived at Young's Point and assumed command and the real work of the campaign and siege of Vicksburg began. The first step was to secure a foothold upon high ground on the east side of the river, from which the troops could operate against Vicksburg. The river was high and rains were incessant and the prospects of making land movements before spring did not seem propitious. The political situation in the North called for a forward movement and the morale of the army required activity, so a number of experiments were attempted in order that the troops should be kept occupied and the people of the North be made to feel that operations were in progress. A canal was dug across the point of land opposite the city of Vicksburg and the levee was cut at Lake Providence, which it was thought would open a water route from the Mississippi through Lake Providence, Bayou Baxter, Bayou Mound and the Tensas, Washita and Red Rivers to the Mississippi. An other opening in the levee was made opposite Helena to Moon Lake to secure a passage through the lake, Yazoo Pass, to the Coldwater and then to the Tallahatchie River where it joins the Yallabusha and forms the Yazoo River. An expedition was sent up the Yazoo River to Steel's Bayou, Black Bayou, Deer Creek, Rolling Fork and into the Big Sunflower River. These experiments consumed time and directed the attention of the Union soldiers, the Confederates and of the Northern people until the river fell and the movement by land could be carried out.

*   *   *

This rather concisely summarizes events during the campaign up until Fred's arrival at his father's headquarters, on March 29, 1863. Fred followed this with an account of his adventures with the army during the campaign, which is considerably shorter than the version he had given in the *National Tribune* in 1887, which follows.

# PART I

# THE MIGHTY GRAPPLE WITH THE STRONGHOLD AT VICKSBURG

## PAST THE BATTERIES THE FLEET SAFELY GUIDES THROUGH FLAME AND SMOKE.[1]

I have always appreciated my good fortune in being placed near my father, and thus allowed to see much of him and most of his able Lieutenants who were engaged in the great struggle for National existence, which continued for four years 1861–'65.

Early in March, 1863, I was made happy by receiving the news from my mother, who was then at Memphis, Tenn., that she would be with me at Covington, Ky., (where I was at school,) very soon, and upon her arrival there she imparted to me a piece of information which I considered very important. She said that my father had consented to have me return with her to Memphis, and that he would give me permission[2] to go from there to Youngs Point[3], to join him with the army, which was then in front of Vicksburg.

Never was a lad more happy than I, when my mother, my two brothers, U. S. Jr., and Jesse—my sister Nellie and I started for Memphis. Upon our arrival there, after a comfortable journey, Col. Hillyer,[4] Provost Marshal of the

---

1  Originally published as Fred D. Grant, "General Ulysses S. Grant: His Son's Memories of Him in the Field: The Mighty Grapple With the Stronghold at Vicksburg. Past the Batteries The Fleet Safely Guides Through Flame and Smoke," *National Tribune*, Jan. 20, 1887, 1.

2  On March 6, 1863, Grant had written Julia, "I want Fred to come and stay with me." Grant, *Papers*, vol. 7, 396.

3  See Appendix II for a short gazetteer of places mentioned in the text.

4  For a short profile of most persons mentioned in the text, see Appendix I. Colonel William S. Hillyer, of Grant's staff, accompanied Fred from Memphis to Young's Point, bringing along his own 10-year-old son, William S. Hillyer Jr. who had already been with his father in the field several times,

A prewar image of Col. William S. Hillyer, Sr., aide-de-camp to U. S. Grant.
*Library of Congress*

District and Aide-de-Camp upon my father's staff, informed me that a beautiful Indian pony had been sent from Illinois by Col. Bowers for my special use while at head-quarters with father. This was the cause of great anxiety on my part to start off immediately to join the army. I had never before possessed a pony, except one which I used for three weeks in the Fall of 1861, while at Cairo, and lost at the Battle of Belmont.[5]

My elders at Memphis were probably willing to indulge me and humor my enthusiasm, or possibly my boyish pranks were tiresome to them, for I was permitted to take the first boat possible that passed down the river. At the time of my starting there were many rumors of attacks having been made upon passing boats at Greenville, and I noticed that the pilot-house of our boat was sheathed in boiler-iron and that the engine was protected in the same way. I was informed that in case of attack I must get under cover on the west side of the boat, for safety. The morning following our departure from Memphis, as we neared Greenville a body of men and one brass gun were seen upon the shore, and some one gave the alarm, "The enemy." I saw a coil of rope upon the cabin deck, and proceeded to climb into the hole in the center of the coil, deeming myself in safe refuge there.

often wearing a private's uniform. Surprisingly, many other officers took young sons on campaign at times during the war, among them John A. McClernand, William T. Sherman, Rutherford B. Hayes, and Rufus King. See Grant, *Papers*, vol. 2, 328.

5 While at Camp Yates, near Quincy, where Grant commanded the 21st Illinois (June 26–July 12, 1861), Fred rode several horses. The pony he mentions was probably the "little pony" Grant lost at Belmont on Nov. 7, 1861, a battle in which, despite the implication of his comment, Fred was not present. See Grant to Jesse Grant, Nov. 27, 1861, in *Letters of U. S. Grant to His Father and Younger Sister, 1857–1878*, ed. Jesse Grant Cramer (New York, 1912), 70.

The USS *Silver Cloud*, a stern-wheel, tin-clad gunboat similar to the vessel escorting Fred.
*Naval History & Heritage Command*

Our convoy being what was called a tin-clad gunboat,[6] and belonging to what was then known as the "Musquito Fleet," [*sic*] went bravely ahead and fired one or two shots at the enemy, but as they were not answered we passed quietly by the dangerous point. Shortly after this some one came across the dock, and seeing me at the heart of the rope-coil, said: "See here, sonny, if them rebs had fired at us and hit our boiler, you would have gone straight up through the hurricane deck, and there would not have been a piece of you left to send to your mamma."

We continued safely along, passing Helena and the great cut at the Yazoo Pass, arriving [March 29th] at Young's Point, where I with joy found my father, who had made his headquarters upon a steamboat which was tied up to the levee.[7] As soon as possible after getting on board my father's boat, I had my precious pony saddled

6  It was not possible to identify the vessel Fred traveled aboard. A "tin-clad" was a river steamboat lightly "armored," usually by heavy wooden beams and cotton bales, with perhaps a little iron covering vital areas, usually "rail road iron," that is iron rails, or boiler plate, and furnished with a few cannon. Information about any warships and other vessels mentioned in these pages is based on James L. Mooney, ed., *The Dictionary of American Naval Fighting Ships* (Washington, D.C., 1959–1991).

7  Where not provided in the original, dates are given in brackets as [March 29th]. Fred arrived on the evening of March 29th. The next day the general wrote Mrs. Grant, "Fred. is looking well and seems as happy as can be at the idea of being here. . . . says he will write twice each week. I will require Fred. to read and study his arithmetic. I will not be able to hear ~~lesson~~ [*sic*] his lessons much however," and expressed regret that their other son, 11-year-old "Buck," had not accompanied Fred. Grant, *Papers*, vol. 7, 490–491.

and bridled, and my father, who wished to go down to see the work that was being done at the canal, kindly allowed me to go with him. He also seemed interested in my pony and my pleasure.

As I remember, just back of the levee where the river strikes against the shore and turns to pass up toward Vicksburg, piles had been driven; in front of these piles was a sheeting of planks, and just back of that the men had dug the canal.[8] This canal was wide enough for the passage of a Mississippi steamer; it was now filled with men hard at work digging out the mud. My father and I passed down the canal for some distance, when my father halted and pointed across the river, where we could see the enemy apparently at work diligently upon a fortification which faced our own canal. Gen. Grant turned to some one near, I think Col. Rawlins, and said: "This will not do; boats cannot pass through this canal even if it is successfully completed."

We then turned and started back to Young's Point, Every spot of ground that was not covered with water between Young's Point and the canal was used for camps by the soldiers. During our ride back to headquarters we visited the quarters of various Generals, and my father had much to say to them upon matters that I did not understand or feel interested in at that time. Upon our arrival at the headquarters boat a flag was put out, and soon after a tug came alongside and my father took me with him over to the gunboat *Benton*, the flagship of Admiral Porter.[9]

My father was received most cordially, and we were conducted to Admiral Porter's room. Very soon the Admiral rang a bell and directed the man who answered it to conduct me over the ship and show me everything of interest or that

8 On March 31, 1863, Grant's engineers began excavating a canal between Duckport Landing, on the Mississippi River, and Cooper's Planation, on Walnut Bayou, at the base of De Soto Point, a "peninsula" formed by a very sharp bend on the Mississippi right across from Vicksburg. An earlier attempt had been abandoned due to malaria. The intent was that the canal would permit riverine traffic to bypass the Vicksburg defenses, permitting Grant to shift forces downstream, cross to the east side of the river, and threaten the city from the south. Progress initially was good, but the Mississippi began to fall, rendering the canal useless, and in any case the Confederates had gotten wind of the plan and were posting new batteries, as noted by Fred above. The canal was abandoned on May 4th. Edwin C. Bearss, with J. Parker Hills, *Receding Tide: Vicksburg and Gettysburg: The Campaigns that Changed the Civil War* (Washington, D.C., 2010), 55–58.

9 A prewar "center-wheel catamaran snagboat," designed to remove obstacles from rivers and harbors, the ship was acquired by the U.S. Navy in late 1861 for conversion into a river gunboat. Entering service in February 1862, the *Benton* displaced 633 tons, could steam at 5½ knots, and was armored with up to 2½ inches of iron, backed by heavy timbers. Called by Porter "an ironclad of remarkable strength," her armament varied over time, but usually comprised some modern 9-inch smoothbore guns and 12-pounder howitzers, plus some older heavier pieces. *Benton* was extensively engaged throughout the war.

The USS *Benton*, one of the most powerful river gunboats of the war, and Porter's flagship.
Wash drawing by Francis Christian Muller, done c. 1900.
*U.S. Naval History and Heritage Command*

would give me pleasure—an attention which I appreciated deeply at the time.[10] I have since understood that it was during the interview which occurred then, during my absence from the room, that my father made the first suggestion and proposal of passing the batteries at Vicksburg, which resulted in the campaign as it was carried out afterward.

We returned late that evening to our headquarters, after this important interview between Admiral Porter and Gen. Grant.

Shortly after [April 1st], a trip was made up the Yazoo with two or three gunboats and one transport. The transport stopped just out of range of the guns at Haines's Bluff, and the gunboats continued with Gen. Grant and Admiral Porter up the river and exchanged a few shots with the enemy.[11]

10 In the 1907 version of his memoirs, Fred adds, "the Admiral, doubtless remembering the old saying that 'little pitchers have long ears,'" offered him the tour of the ship (p. 107).

11 Sherman accompanied Grant and Porter on this reconnaissance. William Farina, *Ulysses S. Grant, 1861–1864: His Rise from Obscurity to Military Greatness* (Jefferson, NC, 2007), 18. According to his father, Fred "was quite disappointed" at being left behind. Grant, *Papers*, vol. 8, 9.

I was compelled to remain with the transport,[12] and went on shore with Capt. Bruce [Breese], of the Navy, when very soon we heard shots, and a bullet passing close to our heads Capt. Bruce and I returned to our boat.[13]

Upon the return of the gunboats, Gen. Grant and Admiral Porter came aboard the transport, upon the hurricane deck of which was a new machine gun, something like the Gatling gun of the present day.[14] It was determined to test this gun, and during the firing of it one of the cartridges exploded and a piece of the metal struck my father on the thumb, making a painful and ugly wound, which caused him much suffering for some weeks and distressed me. After our trip up the Yazoo, headquarters were moved [April 3rd] to a house at Milliken's Bend, a few miles up the Mississippi from Young's Point.[15]

Immediately after this move, all the officers became actively engaged in making preparations for something—apparently a great campaign.[16] Admiral Porter came up to our new headquarters with his fleet.[17] Then transports were taken over, to be placed near the gunboats, all of them loaded with bales of hay to be packed around

12 Fred remained aboard the USS *Ivy*, a 50-ton propellor tug that served as a patrol boat, dispatch vessel, and transport, and had been very heavily engaged as Porter's flagship during the naval attack on Fort Hindman in 1862.

13 Fred misremembered the name of Kidder Randolph Breese, Porter's flag captain.

14 This incident is not mentioned in any of Grant's papers, nor in any book about Grant that could be found. The "machine gun" was the "Union Repeating Gun," designed by Wilson Agar (or Ager) before the war. Nicknamed the "Coffee Mill Gun," it was a single-barrel weapon loaded from a magazine by a crank, firing special .58 Minié-type rounds, a system similar to that of the somewhat later and more famous multi-barreled Gatling gun, with which it is often confused. In 1861, impressed by a demonstration, Lincoln and some senior officers arranged to procure a number of these. Not proving very useful in open combat, in part because no one had thought about *how* to use them, and in part because of technical issues, notably barrel overheating, the Agar guns were relegated to fixed fortifications and a few ships. See "Multi-Firing Weapons of the Civil War," The Collectors Firearms Blog, April 29, 2021, https://www.collectorsfirearms.com/blog/post/multi-firing-guns-of-the-civil-war.html, accessed July 24, 2021; "1860s: Advanced Civil War Weapons," Stolen History Blog, Dec. 6, 2020, https://www.stolenhistory.org/articles/1860s-advanced-civil-war-weapons.169/, accessed July 24, 2021.

15 On April 6th, Grant wrote his wife, "Fred. enjoys himself hugely. His pony gets but little rest.," Grant, *Papers*, vol. 8, 132.

16 During the week or so of preparations for passing the batteries, Fred had the run of the camp. On April 16th, Cpl. Alonzo W. Brown of the 4th Minnesota wrote in his diary, "We saw Fred Grant today riding a pony among the camps with a uniform on. He appeared to be about twelve years old." Alonzo Brown, *History of the Fourth Regiment of Minnesota Infantry Volunteers during the Great Rebellion, 1861–1865* (St. Paul, MN, 1892), 175. Brown later became a captain in the 50th United States Colored Troops.

17 By his own admission, Fred wrote these memoirs without resort to reference material, and the next few paragraphs show it, as events are rather garbled. There were two runnings of the Vicksburg batteries during this phase of the campaign, one on the night of April 16–17 and one on that of April 20–21, and Fred, who witnessed both, has conflated the two.

The Ager "Coffee Mill" gun.
*Library of Congress*

the boilers for their protection. Troops were reviewed, and everything was gotten ready for a move. The men did not know positively where they were to go, but all seemed to feel that they were about to take Vicksburg. Finally, volunteers were called for to man the boats.[18]

I remember that after this call for volunteers I was situated where I saw a Colonel with almost his entire regiment standing in front of headquarters; all of them desired to man the boats. The Colonel was W. S. Oliver, and the regiment

18 According to Porter, "the transports were prepared by packing them well with cotton-bales," and each gunboat and transport had a coal barge or other small vessel lashed to its port side, the one exposed to Confederate fire. Volunteers were required because the civilian crews of the transports were, in Porter's words, "declining to serve," though the pilots were "as a rule, determined to stay by their vessels," and later deemed it a special distinction to have run the batteries. Porter, *Naval History*, 309.

was the 8th Mo.[19] They claimed that they had had some experience in working on boats before, in every position that could be mentioned, from that of Captain to a roustabout. I remember that one of those men, in giving arguments and reasons that he should receive the appointment, said that his feet were worn and sore so that he could not march, and as he must go on the campaign he begged to go upon the boat as far as possible. Their courage was marvelous to me. Many of other regiments volunteered, but most of the men, I believe, belonged to Gen. Logan's Division.

The boats which were to run the blockade, having been thoroughly prepared under the direction of Admiral Porter, were all in readiness. About sundown, on the 16th of April, 1863, Gen. Grant, with his staff, took a steamer at Milliken's Bend and dropped down the river to Young's Point.[20] The night as it came on was very dark, but we had our boat run alongside the *Benton*, and my father and Admiral Porter held a consultation. About 10 o'clock all lights were put out, and our fleet started down the river.

Suddenly a rocket went up from the shore. Then a cannon burst forth from Warrenton, and a shot passed directly in front of our boat. We stopped; a flame sprang lurid from a house at De Soto (a little town opposite Vicksburg): then another on the river front, and soon fires were burning all along the shore, in front of the city, and the water was illumined as by day's brightest sun.[21] There in front of us, steaming down the river, were six gunboats, which looked to me like great black turtles, followed closely by three fragile transports, moving directly toward the batteries of the doomed city.

Soon all the [Confederate] guns on the hills and river front opened up their firing on our little fleet, which went slowly onward. Presently the *Benton* came

---

19 Fred misremembered the regiment. Both the 7th and 8th Missouri were present during the campaign, the 7th in John Logan's division of the Seventeenth Army Corps, and the 8th in Frank Blair's division of the Fifteenth Army Corps. Colonel Oliver commanded the 7th Missouri. Mustering into service in June 1861, with many Irish recruits, the regiment earned the nickname "The Irish Seventh." It saw extensive service in Missouri from 1861 and served under Grant in Mississippi from 1862 through the Vicksburg campaign, after which it performed occupation and security duty in Mississippi, Louisiana, and Arkansas. It mustered out in December 1864, having lost 56 men to combat and 130 to disease. See John Davis Evans, *Silencing the Vicksburg Guns: The Story of the 7th Missouri Infantry Regiment as Experienced by John Davis Evans, Union Private and Mormon Pioneer*, ed. Jerry Evan Crouch (Victoria, BC, 2005).

20 Grant and his party were aboard the *Henry Von Phul*, a side-wheel packet built in 1860 for the St. Louis-New Orleans run, which had been requisitioned by the army as a hospital ship and transport but was serving as the general's temporary headquarters. The ship accidentally burned shortly after the war.

21 Reporting on the running of the batteries, Colonel Oliver wrote, "the enemy fired their signal guns and made light by setting fire to two houses on the Louisiana side, so that when opposite the city it was as light as day on the river, and we could see the men at their batteries and the streets in the city plainly." *O.R.*, XXIV, 1, 565.

The steamer *Henry Von Phul*, from which General Grant, Fred, and their party viewed the
Union ironclads run the Confederate batteries at Vicksburg on April 16–17, 1863.
*Murphy Library Special Collections ARC, University of Wisconsin-La Crosse*

to the turn in the river, and a broadside was sent from her at the batteries of the
enemy. Then the boat following came into action. In less than 10 minutes all six
of our vessels were in the midst of battle, and the scene became grand and terrible
to me. Steaming up very near to the Vicksburg shore, our boats poured their shot
and shell into the city. While the gunboats were thus engaged the three transports
passed by, keeping close to the Louisiana shore. Suddenly one of the three stopped;
a flame shot up from her side. She began to reel and turn in an eddy. This boat
was the *Henry Clay*, and had been set on fire by a hot shot from the Warrenton
batteries, burning and destroyed to the water's edge.[22]

The people of Vicksburg turned out en masse; we could see them assembled
all the way up the side of the hill. There seemed to be great excitement there; every
now and then a cheer would go up from among them. I was on the hurricane deck

22 Fred correctly recounts the loss of the *Henry Clay* during the first running of the batteries. Built
in 1858, the side wheel steamer *Henry Clay* was an unarmed transport, with some vitals "protected"
by compressed cotton bales. According to Porter, the first shell "exploded in the cotton barricades
. . . and almost immediately the vessel was in a blaze; another shell soon after bursting in her hull,
the transport went to pieces and sank" with no serious injury to any of those aboard. Porter, *Naval
History*, 310–311; Porter, *Anecdotes and Incidents of the Civil War* (New York, 1885), 176–178; *Naval
O.R.*, Series I, XXIV, 552, 554, 557, 563, 566–567, 672, 704.

Admiral Porter's fleet running the rebel blockade of the Mississippi at Vicksburg, April 16, 1863.
*Currier and Ives*

of our vessel, keeping at the side of my father during this time, who, by the way, was smoking; but I noticed an intense light in his eyes.[23]

It would be impossible to describe my own feelings in witnessing the scene, but the picture of all that occurred that night can never pass from my mind, so terribly and deeply was I impressed. After the transports passed the batteries the gunboats followed, firing constantly as they moved leisurely along, until all were out of range of the enemy's guns.[24]

23 Fred doesn't mention that also present aboard the *Henry Von Phul* watching the ships run the batteries on April 16th, were his mother and three siblings, as well as Maj. Gen. John Alexander McClernand, with his new bride, Minerva Dunlap McClernand, Lt. Col. James H. Wilson of Grant's staff, and War Department special agent Charles A. Dana, the last two taking turns comforting Fred's youngest brother, Jesse, who was frightened by the noise. In her memoirs, Mrs. Grant wrote "Indeed it was a grand sight. . . . The batteries of Vicksburg poured shot and shell upon the heads of the devoted little fleet, but Porter was there—thank Heaven!—to return broadside for broadside." Julia Dent Grant, *Personal Memoirs*, 112–113; Samuel Carter III, *The Final Fortress: The Campaign for Vicksburg 1862–1863* (New York, 1980), 155–156; Charles A. Dana, *Recollections of the Civil War: With Leaders at Washington and in the Field in the Sixties* (New York, 1899), 36.

24 The fleet commenced running the four mile stretch of batteries at about 11:00 pm on April 16th, with the last ship passing beyond the reach of Confederate fire about two-and-a-half hours later. Porter, *Naval History*, 310; *Naval O.R.*, vol. XXIV, 552*ff.*

Tug "Rumsey," showing barges alongside for protection, when running
the Confederate batteries at Vicksburg, April 20-23, 1863.
*Harper's Weekly*

After the cessation of firing, and all was quiet, our boat was turned about and steamed back to Milliken's Bend, up the river. Gen. Grant seemed much absorbed during our return trip. He sat writing; his staff were gathered around him, talking and telling of all that they had seen during the running of the blockade. As to myself, I was sent to bed. The first step of the campaign had been taken, and proved a success for our army.

Reviewing troops now became the order of the day. How grand and delightful it was to see the long lines of men, with their glittering bayonets. Soon I was to see them in battle, and I was filled with enthusiasm. As quickly as the review of a division or corps was completed the higher officers would come to headquarters, to get their orders, I presume. The following day the same thing would occur, and other divisions would be reviewed.

Some days after the blockade had been successfully run by the gunboats Gen. Grant announced that he intended to go down and visit McClernand; so that early the following morning [April 18th] he started with about eight officers (all of his staff) and myself, with 20 cavalrymen as an escort. We rode across the plantation

Often a thorn in Grant's side, Maj. Gen. John A. McClernand commanded the Thirteenth Army Corps during the campaign, until relieved in June.
*Library of Congress*

upon which our headquarters were now placed, and chose a road that if it had not been built had at least been repaired by the troops to such an extent that it really seemed a new road. That proved to be a very hard day's ride, to me, of 30 miles, through woods and swamps after the termination of the good road. We got through safely, reaching Richmond, La, about 10 or 11 o'clock that night, and [New] Carthage during the afternoon [Apr 19th], finding McClernand there with his corps.

On the road to New Carthage was quite a slough, but the water had fortunately almost all run out of it; across this slough the troops had built a bridge. It was a very narrow one, only wide enough to admit of the passage of one wagon at a time. As the train of troops was passing when we arrived there, and Gen. Grant being unwilling to halt them while we should go over, he turned out to the side of the bridge and made a dash for the opposite bank. His horse did not quite clear the distance, but plunged into the mud at the bottom, and then out again to the other side. It was a daring leap and the rest of us who followed him, not having confidence in our horses, or in our ability to stay on them, stopped on the edge, looked at the slough, and turned to ride tamely over the bridge, following a wagon that was slowly crossing. We were amply repaid for this extra ride, as it gave Col. Rawlins and several others of the staff the opportunity to criticize and swear at a balking mule-team.[25] At another point on the road during this journey, where we had to cross quite a large stream, we stopped in it to allow our horses to drink, when suddenly the horse that Col. Rawlins was riding threw himself down and began to roll. The Colonel walked deliberately out to the opposite shore and clambered up. One of the Orderlies rode forward

25  In a 1907 version of his memoir, Fred says the mule-team gave Rawlins "an admirable opportunity to display a talent which he exhibited on occasions—that of ornamental profanity." Fred used phrases like "ornamental profanity," "said things," and "energetic language" variously in the several versions of his memoir to indicate cursing. See, for example, Fred Grant "Annual Address" (1907), 107.

John A. Rawlins, as a brigadier general, Grant's Chief-of-Staff for most of the war.
*Library of Congress*

to catch the horse. All expected an outburst from Col. Rawlins, who was not in the best of humor, owing to our long, hot and tedious ride, but to every one's surprise we saw him laughing, and heard him say: "Don't touch that horse; every time he turns over he is worth a hundred dollars more." The horse seemed to enjoy his muddy bath, and after splashing about to his satisfaction went ashore, covered with mud and glory. My father, who had given the horse to Col. Rawlins, quietly said: "Rawlins, I am pleased that, according to your reckoning, your horse has increased in value at least twelve hundred dollars."[26] We spent the evening and night of our arrival at New Carthage; father passing most of his time with Gen. McClernand, while the rest of us rode about looking at the camps. At one point we found a crowd of soldiers clustered about a negro, who was singing Southern and old-fashioned slave songs. I remained there listening until the darky sang the "Bonny Blue Flag," when some of the soldiers, becoming indignant, marched the "contraband" off under arrest.[27]

The day following [April 20th] we all returned to Milliken's Bend, where Gen. Grant had a meeting with Gen. Sherman. It was here at father's headquarters that his cook, "Old Shady," sang so often the song which was afterward known so well by the army, and bore his name, "Old Shady."[28] This was the first time I remember to have seen this great General, for whom my father always felt such an admiration.

26 This exchange about the value of the horse reflects the then common belief that such behavior indicated a happy, healthy animal, a little bit of old agricultural lore for which this editor thanks Prof. John Boardman, formerly of Brooklyn College.

27 "The Bonnie Blue Flag," with lyrics by Harry B. Macarthy (1834–1888), was set to Valentine Vousden's 1855 tune "The Irish Jaunting Car." It was one of the most popular Confederate war songs, celebrating secession.

28 This was D. Blakely Durant, a free-born African American, who was a cook for several generals during the war. He often sang "Old Shady," a song celebrating escape from slavery. See Appendix IV for a short profile and the song.

In the course of a few days [April 20th–28th] our headquarters were broken up and we started to join the advanced part of the army, taking our former road through Richmond and part of the way toward New Carthage.[29] We reached the river at a point called "Hard Times" some miles down the Mississippi River. The army having been mostly concentrated below Vicksburg, the next step now necessary was to get them across the river, and to that end reconoissances [sic] were made toward Grand Gulf.

Early on the morning of the 29th of April I saw all the transports lying in front of McClernand's Corps and troops marching aboard them. Soon my father starting off, I keeping near to him, we reached the river bank and boarding a small tug.[30]

The gunboats had already started, and our little tug-boat followed down to within about a mile of the batteries at Grand Gulf. These batteries opened vigorously upon our little fleet, and Admiral Porter responded with vim. After a conflict of some duration with the upper batteries the Admiral dropped down the river with his fleet, where the batteries were engaged with equal vigor for some time; then Admiral Porter returned to the upper batteries, and much to our surprise these opened, firing upon him again; and soon the lower batteries joined in the contest with fresh energy.

Immediately the gunboats formed a line, with their bows toward these upper fortifications, and steamed to within a few hundred yards of them, using their bow guns with effect. I remember distinctly seeing a man jump upon the parapet of the enemy's works just as one of our guns was discharged at them. The shell exploded, apparently, right upon the spot where he was standing, so that he must have been blown to atoms, as he was not to be seen after the explosion and clearing away of the smoke.

After about five hours of fighting, all of which time General Grant and his staff and I spent on board the tug, which was steaming about among the gunboats, we went to the Louisiana shore and landed and walked some distance, after a time finding a road which later on proved of great service. My father and party then

---

29 It was during the night of April 20–21, 1863, that the second running of the batteries by the river fleet took place. Colonel Lagow commanded the transports from the sidewheel transport *Tigress*, which had at various times housed Sherman's headquarters as well as Grant's. Colonel Oliver of the 7th Missouri commanded the *Tigress*, which was crewed by his men. She took heavy damage, but suffered no casualties, and once past the batteries, Oliver beached her below the city. *Tigress* was recovered and returned to service. *O.R.*, XXI, pt. 1, 565ff.

30 On the evening of the 28th, Grant wrote Julia, explaining that on the morrow "Myself, Staff & Fred will be off in a little tug witnessing the Naval attack upon land batteries and the debarkation of troops to carry the heights." Grant, *Papers*, vol. 8, 132. Also present with Grant and Fred on the tug was Radical Republican Congressman Elihu B. Washburne of Illinois, who had met Grant early in the war, and became his staunch supporter, pressing for his promotion and assignment to important posts.

Porter's ironclads engaging Confederate batteries at Grand Gulf, April 29, 1863.
*Naval History and Heritage Command*

returned to the tugboat, which steamed back toward our fleet. Admiral Porter's flagship, the *Benton*, came out to meet us. We all went on board the *Benton* with General Grant, passing through a porthole, near one of the guns. Ah! What a sight met my horrified gaze! Probably the others of our party were more accustomed to such scenes than I, for I was sickened at the scene before me. The deck was covered with blood and pieces of flesh; several dead men, torn and lacerated, lay about us. Some of the gunners, with still bleeding wounds, were standing firmly by their guns.

Admiral Porter had been struck with a piece of shell on the back of his head; his face was colorless and expressed great agony; he leaned forward, using his sword as a cane for support. Gen. Grant told him that he did not believe the transports could be landed in front of the batteries.

The Admiral agreed with him on this point. Although he was suffering, he resolved, with my father, that the gunboats should engage the enemy's batteries that night, and that the transports could run past them during the midst of the bombardment. Our party then returned to Hard Times, and the troops were disembarked.

During the interview which had occurred between my father and Admiral Porter, the latter turned to me and asked if I did not wish to remain with him during the next engagement, saying that he would like to have me, as I might take the place of a gunner he had just lost. The scene around me dampened any ardor I might have possessed for naval glory, so that I replied, trembling lest my father should contradict my statement, that I did not believe my papa would leave me there, even if I wished to stay with the Admiral.[31]

Shortly after our return to the troops we all started on the march. Gen. Grant was at the head of the army with a company of cavalry.[32] As we approached the Mississippi River, toward dusk, after a journey of about six miles, we reached a fine plantation, upon which we saw all the negroes out to receive us. Such a rejoicing there was here! One old white-haired darky sang, in deep and solemn voice, "B'ess de Lord, dey'a comin', comin'," and one would have supposed from the actions of these slaves that they truly believed that the Union soldiers were messengers of the Lord coming among them.[33]

We all stopped on the bank of the river, the troops arriving rapidly. They went into camp as close to the edge of the river as possible. Shortly after sunset was heard the booming of cannon, and in a half hour's time we saw the lights of our transports that were turning at the bend of the river and approaching us quietly, after their successful passage of the blockade. Gen. Grant seemed greatly relieved to find that his transports were safe, and I was relieved to hear his order for "something to eat." During that night a negro came into camp, whom my father questioned, and from whom he learned of a road which led back from Bruinsburg.[34]

---

31 In his 1907 version of his reminiscences (p. 107), Fred wrote "The scene around me dampened my enthusiasm for naval glory, so I replied, 'I do not believe that papa would allow me to serve in the navy.'"

32 Grant's escort was Co. A, 4th Illinois Cavalry. Raised in the summer of 1861, the regiment mustered into service at Ottawa, Illinois, on Sept. 26, 1861. In Nov. of 1861, at Cairo, Illinois, Co. A was detached from the regiment and assigned to escort Grant, which duty it performed until Aug. 1863. Note that the U.S. Army did not use "troop" for a mounted company until after the war.

33 The identity of this plantation seems lost.

34 It was not unusual for African Americans—free or enslaved—to provide valuable intelligence to Union forces. They usually proved reliable sources of information, often having been forced to work on Confederate defenses or having overheard conversations among Confederate officers, who usually spoke freely in front of them. It was common for Union officers to avoid mentioning an African American informant's name, to offer some protection from possible retaliation, using nicknames or code phrases, such as "Black dispatches" or "an intelligent contraband." In this instance, the next day, Grant's troops at Disharoon's plantation began using the boat landing there to embark for the short river crossing to Bruinsburg on the east bank of the river, which had been identified by the unnamed African American as a suitable landing place. Steven E. Woodworth, et al., eds., *The Vicksburg Campaign, March 29–May 18, 1863* (Carbondale, IL, 2013), 162.

# PART II

# THROUGH THE CAMPS. A BOY'S NOVEL ADVENTURES AMONG THE SOLDIERS

## GRANT UNDER FIRE, HIS FEARLESSNESS AT PORT GIBSON AND RAYMOND.[1]

The following morning [April 30th] my father and party went on board a captured rebel gunboat, which was called the *General Price*.[2] As many troops as possible were put on board the gunboats and transports, and all steamed down to where the town of Bruinsburg had been. Not a house was left standing at this place; at least I cannot now remember to have seen one. All had been burned to the ground—dreadful consequence of war! The troops on board were landed and the boats sent back to bring more of them.

I remember that Gen. Grant seemed much gratified at the way in which Admiral Porter cooperated with him in making use of the men-of-war for conveying both infantry and artillery across the river. During that afternoon troops were marched over and placed near the hills back of Bruinsburg, and the boats continued to bring more of them over far into the night, if not until daylight. As there was no great attention paid to me, I laid myself upon the deck of the *Price* and fell into a

---

1 Originally published as Fred D. Grant, "General Ulysses S. Grant: His Son's Memories of Him in the Field: Through the Camps. A Boy's Novel Adventures Among the Soldiers. Grant Under Fire, His Fearlessness at Port Gibson and Raymond," *National Tribune*, Jan. 27, 1887, 1.

2 The *General Price* was a wooden-hulled side-wheel steamboat built in 1856. Acquired by the Confederate navy, she was "armored" with one-inch iron plates backed by 4-inch wooden planking and compressed cotton bales, armed with four 9-inch rifled cannon, and commissioned as the 633-ton gunboat ram CSS *General Sterling Price*. Often engaged with Union vessels while in the Confederate River Defense Squadron, she was sunk in the river during the battle of Memphis (June 6, 1862). Raised and refurbished by the U.S. Navy, she was commissioned as the *General Price* and saw extensive service on western waters until the end of the war.

The USS *General Price*, a former Confederate gunboat taken into Union Service.
*Naval History & Heritage Command*

sound slumber. When I awakened in the morning [May 1st] I discovered that my father was gone.

I could hear the firing of guns, and knew that a battle was in progress. Gen. Lorenzo Thomas, the Adjutant-General of the Army, was still on board the *Price*, and as he seemed to be in charge of all at the landing, I asked him where my father had gone, with the determination to follow him. Gen. Thomas seemed to be very anxious, and said that there was a great battle going on; that my father had left very early in the morning, and had asked him to look out for me, and not allow me, upon any condition, to go on shore.

Upon our return to Bruinsburg, however, where some troops were landed, a rabbit appeared jumping up in the field, and part of a regiment that had just arrived became interested in the pursuit of it.[3] I asked Gen. Thomas to allow me to assist in catching this rabbit. He consented to my doing so. When I reached the soldiers the rabbit had disappeared from view, but fearing that Gen. Thomas would not allow me to come ashore again, I did not return to the boat, but immediately started for the hills to see what was going on at the front.

I soon found a party of men marching down toward the battlefield. I joined them, and had walked several miles, when they were halted. As I felt wearied, and a small train of ammunition wagons at this point was about to start to the front, I

3  In the 1907 version of his memoir (p. 108), Fred identifies this as Colonel Oliver's regiment, the 7th Missouri, which he would encounter again later in the day, in the second paragraph following this.

Brig. Gen. Lorenzo Thomas, Adjutant-General of the U.S. Army, was in charge of recruiting African-American Troops.
*Library of Congress*

made the acquaintance of one of the drivers, who let me ride one of his mules. After some time we reached ground that gave evidence of having been fought upon. There were some wounded men, abandoned canteens, pieces of clothing, etc., strewn about upon the road and field.

We soon came to a fork in the road. At this point a battery of artillery dashed up, and I left my friendly teamster, who had been really kind, having divided his dinner with me. I followed the battery, which went rapidly up to the left-hand road, and was soon brought into action. They were placed upon a hill, at the side of the road, facing the enemy, and opened vigorously with their guns. Not being particularly pleased with the position I had gotten into, I went back to the road, and finding some troops just passing, I joined them. They were soon deployed to the left of the road. My recollection is that these men belonged to the 7th Mo. They moved forward in line of battle and were soon hotly engaged in contest.

While they were there Gen. Grant came along the line, and fearing that he would be displeased to find me here, instead of being on the boat where he had left me, I placed myself behind a tree until he should leave for some other part of the field. He stopped near by, and calling an officer to him, he held some conversation with him and then passed along to the right. Very soon a great shout was heard, and the whole line moved forward. The enemy had given way. I followed with the troops until we reached the road again. The battle was finished, and I was informed that we had carried the day.

Shortly after the battle the troops which I had been with moved a short distance down the road toward Port Gibson, and there went into bivouac about nightfall, and I started off, hoping to find my father, having by this time become

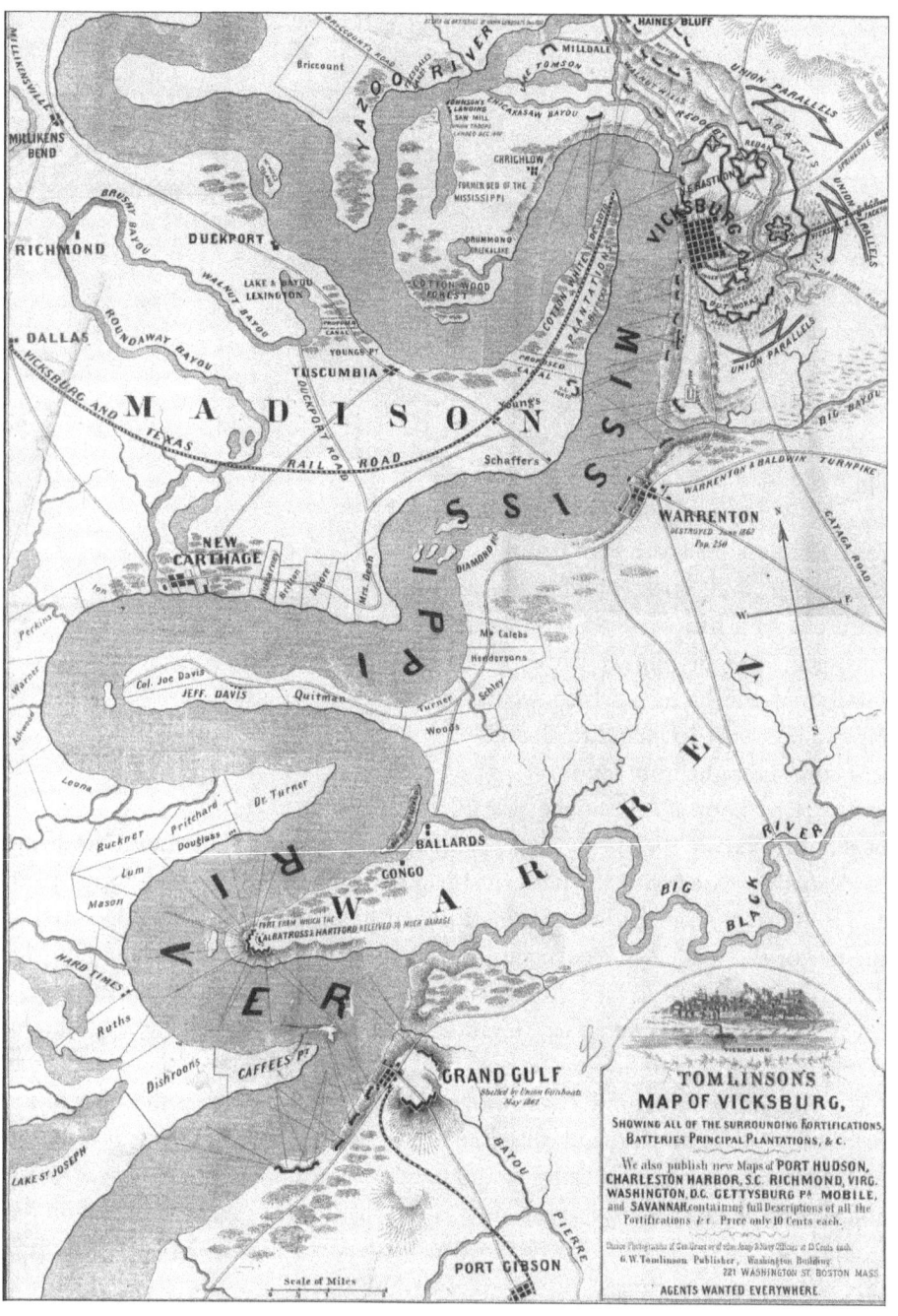

Vicksburg and vicinity.
*Library of Congress*

very tired and hungry. Wherever I went I found dead and wounded men. I was filled with horror as I wandered about over the field.

I came upon burial parties who were collecting the dead and the suffering ones. They would take up a body, carry it back a short distance, and then place it with others upon the ground. They had arranged two lines of dead bodies, one of Union soldiers and one of the enemy's men. This ghastly sight was so frightful to me that I started off and joined another party who were collecting the wounded, and followed them a distance of about a quarter of a mile, to a small log house which had been taken and arranged for a hospital.

Here the Surgeons were occupied in amputating limbs and binding up wounds, and all about the house were poor fellows lying, many of them shrieking with pain from their injuries, and many terrible moans and sights had I to confront now, so that I was really overcome and felt faint and ill. I tottered to the edge of the space occupied by the wounded, and sat, propping myself against a tree, probably the most woebegone twelve-year-old lad in America.

I had not been here long before I saw a soldier on horseback approaching. He stopped in front of me and said, with great surprise, "Why, hello! is that really you?"

I saw with great relief that he was one of my father's Orderlies. He immediately dismounted, came and sat down beside me. I confided to him that I was tired out and felt ill. He then unsaddled his horse, spreading the blanket out and, giving me his saddle for a pillow, said kindly, "Now try to get some sleep." I gratefully lay down, and was soon soundly slumbering, dreaming, however, much of the horrors of war and all that I had seen that day. Later in the night I was awakened by my good friend, the Orderly, who exclaimed: "Look here; your father has come."

I raised myself up and saw, about 50 yards off in the distance, a group of officers, and among them my father. I startled with great joy to him, and I still have in my mind a vivid picture of him as he was then, sitting upon a little camp-stool, drinking from a huge tin cup some coffee which the soldiers had just made for him. As I neared him he looked at me with great surprise, and said: "Why, Fred, I thought I left you safe on the boat at the landing!"

To this I answered, "Yes, sir; you did."

"Then how did you manage to get here?"

I explained all, saying I had walked part of the way. He smiled and replied: "Very well; you cannot get back now, I suppose," and then he continued conversation with officers about him.

My father used to tell the story of my meeting him at the battle of Port Gibson, long afterward, with interest, and much greater satisfaction than he expressed to me that night.

After the coffee had been disposed of, some one came up and said to Gen. Grant that there was an abandoned house less than a half mile up the road, and he immediately started with his staff and took possession of the place for that night.[4] We found in the vacant house a table all arranged for dinner—a choice dinner, too—which the family owning the place had probably left suddenly, owing to the awful battle which had raged so near about them. All of our party sat down comfortably to enjoy a repast which proved to be the only good one that my father partook of during that campaign. Now, however, I may recall the real misery I endured during that night; for being an exhausted, sleepy boy, I took my place on the floor to rest before the officers retired. My father, seeing me peacefully sleeping, and not wishing to disturb me, left me where I was.

When all had left the room shortly after, I was awakened by a dog which came running in, having evidently broken loose from his kennel, or house, and he went around me with his chain dangling after him, searching everywhere for his master. In my inexperience I feared to arouse his anger by getting up to drive him out, and spent a great part of the night veering my feet in the direction of the dog, in place of my head, and he seemed possessed with the idea of investigating me thoroughly and my surroundings. Fortunately he proved not savage, and, with the exception of keeping me awake and uncomfortable all night, did no harm.

The following morning [May 2nd] there seemed to be a great question over transportation, as there were really not enough horses to accommodate all at headquarters. A soldier solved the problem for some of us; he brought in two white horses, very large ones, which had been captured the previous day with some artillery. Mr. C. A. Dana, who was then Assistant Secretary of War, and accompanying my father, took one of these horses, and the other was given over to me.[5] Mr. Dana was well equipped, having a bridle and saddle. Such was not the case with me, and I was compelled to improvise a harness. I made use of an old

---

4  It was perhaps at this house that Fred acquired a small child's picture Bible, which he inscribed to his sister, "Nelle Grant from her brother Fred, May 2, 1863," to which a different hand added "This book was captured the morning after the Battle of Port Gibson." When Fred was wounded in the battle of the Big Black River Bridge, he lost the Bible. Someone found it, and nearly a century later it was in the hands of Mrs. Elizabeth S. Jackson of Washington, D.C. In 1960, during the Civil War Centennial observances, she returned it to Fred's son, Maj. Gen. U. S. Grant III, chairman of the Civil War Centennial Commission. See "Relic Comes Home," *100 Years After* 3, no. 3 (March 1960): 1.

5  Charles A. Dana, then 43, was actually a special agent of the secretary of war to report on military operations in the Western Theater, who became assistant secretary of war after the fall of Vicksburg; see Appendix I. In his memoirs Dana wrote of his meeting with Fred: "While trailing along after the Union forces I came across Fred Grant, then a lad of thirteen, who had been left asleep by his father on a steamer at Bruinsburg, but who had started out on foot like myself as soon as he awoke and found the army had marched. We tramped and foraged together until the next morning, when some officers who had captured two old horses gave us each one. We got the best bridles and saddles we could, and

rope clothes line for my bridle, and the tree of an old side or lady's saddle, without stirrups, completed my outfit.[6] My horse proved to be so slow in movement that I was unable to keep up with Gen. Grant and his staff, so I fell far back in the rear.

The soldiers seemed to be intensely amused at seeing me. As I passed along, a rather small boy upon an old white horse, which was at least 17 hands high,[7] equipped as this one was, I must have been a comical spectacle, and the soldiers cheered me heartily as I went riding by them.[8] But many a mount became as grotesque as mine was then before that campaign was ended.

The distance from our resting-place of the previous night to Port Gibson was only about two miles, but it took me at least three-quarters of an hour to make the trip. I found Gen. Grant upon the bank of Bayou Pierre, where a pioneer company of sappers and miners were building a bridge under the direction of one of his staff officers, Col J. H. Wilson. They were using boards which they stripped from a house near by for materials to construct the bridge.

After remaining here for some time my father and party returned to the town, stopping at the house of a Hebrew friend, who invited us to dine with him.[9] While here my father received the news of Grierson's very successful raid.[10] During this

---

thus equipped made our way into Port Gibson." Charles A. Dana, *Recollections of the Civil War: With Leaders at Washington and in the Field in the Sixties* (New York, 1899), 45.

6 In his *Memoirs*, Fred's father wrote "they were mounted on two enormous horses, grown white with age, each equipped with dilapidated saddles and bridles." Grant, *Personal Memoirs*, vol. I, 487.

7 A "hand" is a measure of horse's height, equal to 4 inches. The height is measured from the ground to the "withers," the area above the shoulders where the neck reaches the back. So at 68 inches or more—5 feet 8 inches or more, or close to 1.8 meters—Fred's "steed" was quite tall, especially for a 12-year-old.

8 A few days later, a visit to nearby Brierfield, the plantation of Confederate President Jefferson Davis, and Hurricane, that of Davis's older brother, Joseph Emory Davis, provided Fred with a "Shetland pony whose prominently ugly appearance provoked the general's [i.e. Grant's] mirthful criticism, notwithstanding the beast was 'Fred's Beauty.'" Brierfield became a hospital and supply depot for the Union, while Hurricane was burned. See Theodore Davis, "Grant Under Fire," *The Cosmopolitan: A Monthly Illustrated Magazine* 14, no. 3 (Jan. 1893): 336–337. No relation to the Confederate president, Theodore R. Davis (1840–1894) was a war correspondent and artist for *Harpers Weekly*, which featured many of his pictures. He later covered the Indian wars and designed new White House china for President Hayes.

9 The identity of this person seems lost.

10 "Grierson's Raid": To deceive the Confederates of his plan to run transports past the Vicksburg batteries and then shift troops south of the city, Grant laid on a number of diversionary actions, the most important of which was a raid by some 1,700 cavalry under Col. Benjamin H. Grierson (see Appendix I), from La Grange, Tennessee, across central Mississippi, to Baton Rouge, Louisiana. Covering some 800 miles in 17 days (April 1–May 2, 1863), save for a few skirmishes, Grierson eluded pursuing Confederate troops and inflicted considerable damage on local infrastructure and morale, but most importantly drew attention from Grant's movements. The 1959 motion picture *The Horse Soldiers* is very loosely based on the raid. See Timothy B. Smith's excellent *The Real Horse Soldiers: Benjamin Grierson's Epic 1863 Civil War Raid Through Mississippi* (El Dorado Hills, CA, 2018).

(Left) Maj. Gen. John Logan. (Right) James H. Wilson, as a major general.
*Library of Congress*

dinner several general officers of our army came in; among them was Gen. Logan. Gen. Grant, after telling these officers of what he had heard of Grierson's success, turned to Logan and complimented him cordially upon the splendid action of his division during the day previous, and told him that he wished him to go to the old railroad suspension bridge below Port Gibson to secure the crossing.[11]

Gen. Logan was apparently pleased at this opportunity of having additional work to accomplish. He turned to me and said: "Come, my boy, and I will show you the prettiest fight you will ever see."

I went with Gen. Logan, who was very enthusiastic, and he fulfilled his promise to have a fight so far as possible for him to do so with an enemy that ran

---

11 Completed in 1860, this suspension bridge crossed Bayou Pierre at Grindstone Ford, near Port Gibson. Retreating Confederates tried to burn it on May 2nd, but Union troops soon doused the fire and repaired it. Brig. Gen. Marcellus M. Crocker's division began crossing; "The Bridge at Bayou Pierre Loss in Skirmishing," *New York Times*, May 23, 1863, 1.

Col. Benjamin Grierson
*Harper's Weekly*

away after a few shots were fired. I returned to Port Gibson after the skirmish at the suspension bridge, and found my father gone, the bridge at the Bayou Pierre finished and our army crossing. I followed the troops until dark, when they halted and went into bivouac.

I rode on until I reached the crossing of the North Fork, where the troops were constructing another bridge. I stopped at a house near by, which had a porch in front, covered over with sleeping officers. I crawled in between two of them, both of whom awoke and in energetic language remonstrated with me. I told them

Maj. Gen. John B. Sanborn
*National Archives*

who I was, when one of them, Col. (afterward General) J. B. Sanborn,[12] welcomed me kindly and loaned me part of his overcoat for a pillow. I remained there until nearly dawn, when, becoming very cold, I got up and went indoors. There I found a bed with two occupants, and I took the liberty of finding a place of rest between them. The next morning when I awoke I found that my bedfellows were two large negroes. I had slept well, but had thought my quarters close.

On the morning of May 3 I passed on from my resting-place and found my father at the bridge watching troops who were crossing the North Fork. I suppose I looked badly, as father asked me if I felt ill. I explained to him that the horse I had used the day before had been a poor one and had fallen down and injured my leg badly, so that I felt very stiff and tired.[13] He replied kindly that I must use the one he had ridden, which was a horse belonging to Gen. A. J. Smith. All of my father's horses had been left on the west bank of the Mississippi River. We soon mounted our horses, I taking the one father proposed for me to have, and all started for Hankinson's Ferry.

After riding a few miles my father and staff went ahead of the troops, and we soon came to where the road forked, and found that the enemy had placed there some artillery and infantry in line of battle. Gen. Grant sent a messenger back to the troops to hasten them forward, and a skirmish-line was formed by the men

12 Sanborn (see Appendix I) said of his encounter with Fred, "In a half-conscious state, the impression was made upon my mind that some intruder was punching my back with his knees and elbows. To such an extent did this proceed, that, being fully aroused, I made a great effort to expel the fellow, at the same time asking 'Who are you?' and a boyish or childish voice answered back 'I am Fred Grant; I am cold.' A large robe was furnished, and greater quiet followed." Brown, *History of the Fourth Regiment of Minnesota Infantry*, 187.

13 Despite Fred's injury, that same day Grant wrote Julia, "Fred is very well, enjoying himself hugely. He has heard balls whistle and is not moved in the slightest by it. He was very anxious to run the blockade of Grand Gulf." Grant, *Papers*, vol. 8, 155.

Brig. Gen. Andrew Jackson Smith commanded a division in the Thirteenth Army Corps.
*Library of Congress*

he had with him. We could see what appeared to be a large body of the enemy marching up the road from Grand Gulf and passing on toward Hankinson's Ferry. Gen. Logan soon reached the front, with two regiments of his division. These regiments were put in order for battle and moved forward, the enemy soon giving way before them, and we resumed our journey to Grand Gulf.

After this skirmish, in which we lost one man killed and several wounded, our escort in moving down the road picked up many muskets and about 30 prisoners. All these we took into Grand Gulf with us. When we arrived Admiral Porter had reached there, and Gen. Grant went immediately on board the *Benton*, several others following him. I remember well the cordial manner of the Admiral when he invited us to stay with him. He at this time gave my father a package of letters, among which, I have since learned, was one from Gen. Banks, saying that he could not be at Port Hudson as soon as he was expected there, and that he would have with him fewer men than Gen. Grant had counted upon his having. This, I presume, necessitated a change of orders; at any rate Gen. Grant began immediately to write letters and orders to his different Generals. He continued steadily upon this work until about 2 o'clock[14] in the morning [May 4th], when he borrowed a change of linen[15] from one of the naval officers (his own having been left and forgotten in his anxiety upon graver subjects), then ordering his horse he started for McPherson's command. I was left by my father with Col. Lagow, of the staff, and the next day [May 5th] one of the transports reached us, bringing our baggage and horses on board of it.

14 Ed Bearss says that Grant and Fred spent the night of May 4th at the home of Mrs. Samuel Pipes Bagnell, a mile north of Hardscrabble Crossroads, on the Port Gibson-Vicksburg Road. Bearss, *Receding Tide,* 146–147.

15 That is, Grant borrowed some clean underwear.

Maj. Gen. James B. McPherson,
Seventeenth Army Corps commander.
*Library of Congress*

The following afternoon Col. Lagow started with wagons of our headquarters to join the army, taking me with him. We reached my father at a little town called Rocky Springs, where he had taken possession of an old Masonic Lodge for his headquarters.

The next day [May 6th] Gen. Sherman came up with the Fifteenth Corps. By the time of his arrival Gen. Grant had gone on some distance, and when Gen. Sherman joined him, we were all seated on the porch of a very large, comfortable house. My father greeted him pleasantly, but Gen. Sherman seemed agitated; I think because of the wagons on the road, which interfered with the progress of his troops. Gens. Grant and Sherman walked up and down the porch talking for some time. When they had finished their conversation, Gen. Sherman seemed relieved and more cheerful. He soon departed.

From the 7th until the 12th of May my father spent his time, it seemed to me, riding in every direction, staying a short time with each of his three corps commanders, Sherman, McClernand and McPherson. All the time was passed in following my father about, by us at headquarters, and his "mess" began to be so neglected that I decided to take my meals with the soldiers, who did a little foraging on the road and lived much better than the commanding General. My father's table at this time was, I may frankly say, the worst I ever saw or partook of. Even in times of peace he cast little thought upon his appetite and fare.

On the 12th day of May, as we approached Fourteen Mile Creek, the enemy opened fire upon us. Osterhaus, who commanded the advance division upon the road on which we were moving, was ordered to throw a regiment out as skirmishers to the left, and send some cavalry on the road and on to the right. After a skirmish which continued probably an hour the enemy left our front, but we could hear

Brig. Gen. Peter J. Osterhaus commanded a
division in the Thirteenth Army Corps.
*Library of Congress*

the roar of artillery away off to our right, so we knew a battle was going on somewhere in that direction.

I had become very friendly with one of the Orderlies near me, called "Pony."[16] After the enemy had departed from our immediate front Pony and I crossed the creek and rode out a distance of probably a mile. We saw some of the rebels, with one cannon. We, fearing that they would take us prisoners, started on a road to the right and in the direction of the cannonading, that we could still hear.

Going up this road for possibly half a mile, we saw 10 or 12 horses tied to a fence in front of a house near by. Pony immediately proposed that he and I should make an independent charge upon them and capture the horses while their riders were indoors, and if possible try to surprise the men themselves into a surrender to us. This was a bold move, but we made ready and started off at full speed. I was armed with a small pistol and Pony with the equipment of a cavalry soldier.[17] The idea suddenly entered my head that possibly so many men might make prisoners of us.

I conveyed my thoughts to Pony. "Yes, we are in a scrape, but it is too late to turn back now," he said. We went on with apparent courage but much trepidation in our hearts to take possession of the horses, when some one came rapidly out of the house. He was uniformed in blue, and we found with grateful feelings that we had been trying to capture an advance detachment of the signal corps of General Sherman's command. Pony seemed greatly chagrined at being placed in the ridiculous position in which we now appeared, but I was satisfied and happy to find myself with friends instead of being in the hands of the enemy. We did

16 Unless William Silliman Hillyer Jr. is meant, "Pony" cannot be identified.

17 This mention of "a small pistol" is the only time in any version of Fred's memoirs that he indicates he was armed, at least some of the time.

Brig. Gen. Marcellus M. Crocker
*William L. Clements Library*

the best we could under the existing circumstances, and joined our friends of the torch and flag at dinner.[18]

When dinner was over the firing had ceased in the direction of Raymond, and we started upon our return to our headquarters; but when we got back to the main road we found pickets stationed there, and we had some difficulty in convincing them that we were friends wishing to return to the Union lines. We passed that night at an old farmhouse,[19] and the following day [May 13th], rode into Raymond.

The battle of Raymond was fought by two divisions of McPherson's Corps, commanded by Gens. John A. Logan and M. M. Crocker, two soldiers as gallant as ever drew sword. Logan, being senior, commanded during the fight. To see Logan on the field was worth a great deal of one's life. He was called by his troops "Fighting Jack," and they were thoroughly devoted to him. Crocker, who was also very brave, was not as handsome as Logan, but his troops swore by him. No division stood better than his in battle, nor was there one better in assault than his (Crocker's). When we arrived upon the ground over which the battle of Raymond had been fought, we saw how desperate the contest had been; at least along that part of the road upon which we approached, for the wreck of battle had not yet been removed.

All the fearful sights were in plain view except the wounded, who had been carried by sympathizing comrades to the town. Whether or not the number of Surgeons was sufficient I cannot say, but when we came to a house that was occupied by the Confederates as a hospital my father sent them Dr. Hewitt, of his

18 The phrase "our friends of the torch and flag" refers to the signalmen, who used flags by day and torches by night to send messages.

19 This was apparently Dillon's Plantation, about seven miles west of Raymond.

The battle of Raymond.
*Library of Congress*

staff, to attend to their wants, and gave directions for medical supplies to be left for them.[20] I remember that several times, later on during the siege of Vicksburg, my father sent food and medical stores back to Raymond, and at one time he sent again Dr. Hewitt to care for the sick; and that officer must have been taken prisoner, for he did not return to headquarters again during the siege.

We spent a night at Raymond, and next morning [May 14th], in a driving storm, we started for Jackson, the Capital of Mississippi. This city is about 17 miles from Raymond. After proceeding about 15 miles, we were passing through a dense woods when a shot was fired. Some one of the staff shouted:

"General, the sharpshooters are aiming at you."

All of us stopped and turned about, except my father, to get under cover. Gen. Grant directed his horse to the side of the road and dashed into the woods directly toward the place whence the bullets were coming. He was quickly followed by Cols. Wilson and Lagow, and they by half a dozen Orderlies. Soon the whole of the escort went in, forming a skirmish-line and moving straight forward until

20 On the adventures of Dr. Hewit (one "t"), see Appendix I.

Brig. Gen. James M. Tuttle commanded a division in the Fifteenth Army Corps.
*Library of Congress*

we arrived at a large house, where we were halted.[21]

Shortly after this Gen. Sherman's Corps came up, when some regiments were thrown out as skirmishers and moved forward some distance. Sherman himself soon arrived and began to place his men in line of battle; when they were all up and in position they were moved forward. We then followed this line, with slight skirmishing, until we reached a hill with an open field before it.

Away off to our left we could see McPherson and the enemy forming in lines of battle. Soon they were engaged in close contest. Sherman had now advanced against the line of fortifications about the city, halting for a short time when close up before them to take position for the assault. In the meantime we could hear the guns booming away on our left. Gen. Tuttle, of Gen. Sherman's Corps, was sent to our right. During the time that Gen. Sherman's men were being posted he himself was with Gen. Grant on the porch of an old house near by.

Suddenly all the guns in our front opened upon us, and our line was broken, the men making for the rear. Both Gens. Grant and Sherman immediately mounted their horses and, riding among the soldiers soon stopped them and made them return to their lines and prepare for battle.

My father, giving some directions to Gen. Sherman, rode off to that part of the field where Tuttle was engaged. I followed, and we soon came to where Tuttle's Division was forming in line in the midst of a very dense forest. This division was moved forward, and coming to the edge of the woods they found there the enemy's breastworks confronting them. The whole division dashed forward, going over the works without meeting great resistance. The gallant men were then wheeled

---

21 Fred had by this time apparently been under fire on several occasions, but here he rather casually mentions that he had taken part in an advance under fire.

to the left and started up the line of the enemy's intrenchments, Gen. Grant accompanying them. I, thinking the battle was ended, rode off toward the town, going directly to the State-house. When I arrived at the Capitol the Confederate troops were passing. They were in haste and paid no heed to my presence, although I wore a blue uniform.[22] I was very small, very wet, much splashed with mud, and altogether unattractive. I was the only "Yankee" around.

Soon after the retreating Confederates had passed I looked up the street in the direction from which they had come and discovered some one on horseback carrying the Union flag approaching. This man rode past me and, stopping at the Capitol, dismounted and entered. I was filled with great enthusiasm, followed him to the second floor of the building and passed through an open door. It proved to be the Governor's room which I entered. A consultation must just have taken place there, for the table was covered with papers and several pipes were lying about, the smoke still issuing from one of them. I took what I supposed to be the Governor's pipe, as it was the handsomest one and lying upon one end of the table. I believe that the Governor and his friends had left in great haste, when they saw their defenders retreating.

When I had looked about until quite satisfied, I returned to the street, and looking up I saw the officer whom I had accompanied into the building up high in the dome or cupola of the Capitol raising the Union flag over this fallen city. As there have been several people who have each claimed to have been the one who raised our flag over the Capital of Mississippi, I may describe the officer's appearance as I saw him perform this famous act.

He was a rather stout man, about five feet seven or eight inches in height, with very dark complexion, black hair, eyes and beard. He wore his beard long and full. From his uniform I supposed him to be a Captain, although he may have been a First Lieutenant. He must have anticipated some opposition to his enterprise, for when I rode up to meet him he avoided me, paid no heed to my salutations,

---

22 In an interview years later, Fred said that he had several times pestered his father for a commission, which the general naturally refused, and went on to say that shortly before the capture of Jackson, "Gov. Yates of Illinois was visiting my father and I got the Governor to promise [me] a commission, but my father wouldn't allow it. Some of the soldiers sewed a pair of captain's shoulder straps on my blue coat, and naturally I felt then as if I were running the war. However, the Paymaster did not take cognizance of my rank and dignity." "Gen. Grant's Career," *New York Times*, April 12, 1912, 2. Fred apparently wore the captain's bars regularly; on May 26, 1863, Emilie Riley McKinley, a staunchly secessionist, albeit northern-born teacher on a plantation near Vicksburg, wrote in her diary, "His son [*i.e.*, Fred], a boy of 12 years, was at headquarters. He was a good-natured looking boy—not smart. He ranks as a captain on his father's staff." Emilie Riley McKinley, *From the Pen of a She-Rebel: The Civil War Diary of Emilie Riley McKinley*, ed. Gordon A. Cotton (Columbia, SC, 2001), 18, 76n.

Gen. Joseph E. Johnston, commander of
Confederate forces in the Western Theater.
*Library of Congress*

and darted past to gain the door of the Capitol. He proved to be Colonel Cornelius Cadle.[23]

After leaving the State-house I remounted my pony and rode some distance toward the west, where I saw some horsemen advancing. They proved to be Gen. Grant with his staff and escort.[24] I returned with them to the city, where we went to a hotel called the Bowen House;[25] my father having the rooms given him that had been occupied by the Confederate General Joseph E. Johnston the previous night.

After a refreshing bath my father went down to the balcony of the hotel. There were assembled a few people, and the street in front of the building was crowded with negroes and some white persons. Presently an officer attired in Confederate uniform, with a flushed face, pushed his way upon the porch, and approaching my father, said something disagreeable, or intended to be so. My father told him to leave instantly, but as the officer refused to do so, Gen. Grant went to the railing

23 Though Cadle was present, the officer who actually raised the colors of the 59th Indiana over the Mississippi state capital at Jackson was Capt. Lucien B. Martin (1831–1898) of the 4th Minnesota, from Brig. Gen. Sanborn's staff.

24 In the *New York Times* interview published in 1912, Fred said that when his father rode up to the state capital, "I told him that I wanted the credit for capturing Jackson. He didn't think it was much of a joke, but the men, who made sort of a pet of me, laughed about it." "Gen. Grant's Career," 2. Fred was accompanied in the "capture" of the capitol by *New York Herald* correspondent Sylvanus Cadwallader (1825–1908), who described him as the "stout, good hearted son of the general." Sylvanus Cadwallader, *Three Years with Grant, As Recalled by War Correspondent Sylvanus Cadwallader,* ed. Benjamin P. Thomas (New York, 1955), 73–75.

25 Built in 1857, the Bowman House—not Bowen—was the largest hotel in Jackson, a four-story brick structure with some 100 rooms, insured for $35,000. Reputedly the best hotel in Mississippi, many delegates to the state's secession convention had stayed there in 1861. It housed Joseph E. Johnston's headquarters until hastily evacuated on the morning of April 14th, was reoccupied after Union troops withdrew, and burned down accidentally in June 1863. Mary Carol Miller, *Lost Landmarks of Mississippi* (Jackson, 2002), 42–49.

of the porch, and calling up to him Serge's Spades,[26] of his escort, ordered him to arrest this officer. The man obstinately refused to move, when Serge's Spades drew his saber, and said: "Now go, or I will run you through."

The officer retired thus under arrest, or guard. I never forgot this Confederate's face, so excited was I over the incident, and when I saw him nine years after, in the Khedive's (Ismail Pasha's) service in Egypt, I recognized him instantly.[27] The circumstances just related were recalled, and we talked over the affair; and he took occasion to say to me that he had ever felt grateful to my father for the leniency shown him, when the punishment might have been so much more severe.

26 Sgt. Commodore C. Spaids, of Co. A, 4th Illinois Cavalry, Grant's escort company. See Appendix I.

27 From November 1871 through September 1872, Fred, then a second lieutenant in the 4th Cavalry, was an aide-de-camp to William T. Sherman for most of the general's tour of Spain, southern France, Italy, Malta, Egypt, Constantinople, Russia, Germany, Austria, Switzerland, Northern France (where Fred departed to visit Denmark), and the UK. While in Egypt they met some of the 50 or so former Union and Confederate officers, including several generals, who were in Egyptian service. Unfortunately this officer cannot be identified. William T. Sherman, *The Memoirs of General W. T. Sherman*, 2 vols. (New York, 1885), 2:476.

# PART III

# FIGHTING JACK LOGAN, HOW THE SOLDIERS WERE INSPIRED BY HIS EXAMPLE

## GRANT'S MIGHTY GRIP, "I'LL CAPTURE VICKSBURG IF IT TAKES ME THIRTY YEARS!"[1]

After an early dinner at our hotel was over the officers of high rank began to come in to talk over matters of importance and get all their instructions. About the middle of that afternoon Gens. Grant and Sherman, with their respective staffs, went out for inspection of the city of Jackson. They soon came upon a large shed containing 2,000 bales of cotton marked C.S.A. It was decided that Col. Lagow should be ordered to fire the cotton, and it made a tremendous blaze. It seemed to me that in less than two minutes the flames went up a distance of a hundred yards.

We then visited a factory where they were manufacturing cotton cloth. After our going through this building the operators were called together and they were told to take out what they wanted and leave the building, as it was to be destroyed. They all gathered up some of the cloth and streamed out in a line into the street. We did not see this factory destroyed, but went on to Pearl River, where there was a good bridge.[2]

---

1  Originally published as Fred D. Grant, "General Ulysses S. Grant: His Son's Memories of Him in the Field: Fighting Jack Logan; How the Soldiers Were Inspired by His Example. Grant's Mighty Grip, 'I'll Capture Vicksburg if it Takes Me Thirty Years!'" *National Tribune*, Feb. 3, 1887, p. 1.

2  The cotton mill belonged to brothers Joshua and Thomas Green. In his memoirs, Grant wrote "The proprietor visited Washington while I was President, to get his pay for his property, claiming it was private. He asked me to give him a statement of the fact that his property had been destroyed by National troops, so that he might use it with Congress, where he was pressing, or proposed to press, his claim. I declined." Grant, *Personal Memoirs*, I:506–507. Congress rejected the Green's petition in 1873. Other parts of Jackson were burned, but as was the case in other cities, many of the fires were started by the retreating Confederates destroying military supplies or by local looters. See

A battery was placed on the bank and the piers knocked down. The superstructure soon fell into the river. Father then conversed with Sherman as to what should be destroyed so that Jackson should not be used as a military depot. He then returned to the hotel, where we remained until the middle of the following afternoon. During our stay in this city I remember one man who was brought in as a prisoner in whom I took an interest. This person had a conversation with Gen. Grant, but was not treated as almost all prisoners were, and was soon dismissed.[3] I learned afterward that he had come as a bearer of dispatches from Johnston to Pemberton. Now orders began to be sent out in every direction.

The following day, May 15, my father started off in the direction of Vicksburg.[4] This was the first time I had had the opportunity of being in the rear of such a large part of the army. Our transportation was the source of great amusement to all. We passed a train that was composed of every conceivable kind of vehicle except what was prescribed by army regulations. First a carriage, drawn by an ox and a mule, loaded with soldiers and knapsacks and cooking utensils. Then we saw an old cotton-wagon, drawn by a pair of horses, a pair of oxen, with a donkey in the lead, the wagon being loaded with provisions. Next came a negro driving a vehicle containing a negress (some one's cook) with four or five pickaninnies. Then followed a cart drawn by a horse in the shafts and a donkey in the lead—a tandem team. We rode as far as Clinton, a small town about 12 miles out from Jackson, where we stopped over for the night. At Clinton my father appeared contented, as if he thought most of the work of the campaign was finished, and for the first time since the beginning of the campaign he joined in the general conversation with his staff and those about him. Although I was too young to fully appreciate all that was said then, I remember well that Edwards's [sic] Station was mentioned by the officers, and that a battle was expected to occur there two days later, May 17, and that it was hoped would finish the great campaign. I went to sleep that night in the room my father occupied, and after quietly resting for some time I was awakened by a great knocking at the door. I do not know at what hour exactly this took place.

---

Cadwallader, *Three Years with Grant*, 75; Sherman, *Memoirs*, I:321–362; Bearss and Grabau, *Battle of Jackson*, 30.

3 The "man who was brought in as a prisoner" was probably Charles S. Bell, a Union spy serving undercover in the Confederate Army. He gave Grant a copy of Joe Johnston's directive to Pemberton to unite their armies, which prompted Grant to order McPherson to move his troops to prevent the juncture, precipitating the battle of the Big Black River on May 17th. See Appendix I.

4 When Grant, Sherman, McPherson, and their entourages left the Bowman House on the morning of May 16th, the proprietor demanded payment for use of his rooms, whereupon one of his entourage, either War Department special agent Charles A. Dana or Lt. Col. James H. Wilson, cheerfully handed him a Confederate $100 bill. Cadwallader, *Three Years With Grant*, 75; Brooks D. Simpson, *Ulysses S. Grant: Triumph Over Adversity, 1822–1865* (Boston, 2000), 198.

My father got up, lighted his candle, and going to the door found one of his Aids there, Col. C. B. Lagow, who announced a "messenger from McPherson." The soldier was brought to the door, and delivered to my father a letter. After reading it through carefully, Gen. Grant looked up and uttered an exclamation of surprise. The envelope was given back to the soldier as the receipt for delivery of the letter, and Col. Lagow was ordered to have all in readiness to start for the front at an early hour in the morning. My father went back to bed and was soon quietly asleep.

The next morning, the 16th of May, was bright and beautiful. We were ready to start very early, and after partaking of a light breakfast all mounted our horses, all trying to keep up with Gen. Grant, who rode very rapidly to the front, the rest of us following. Soon many of the staff were left behind. Cols. Wilson and Lagow and I, approaching Champion's farm, began to hear the firing of scattered musketry, and then the boom of artillery. We reached the bend of the road, where the troops were, about a half mile beyond the farm, and found them engaged in the heaviest kind of a battle.

Soon all the staff officers arrived at this point, and Rawlins was sent to McClernand, who was on our left (the division we were with then was commanded by Gen. Hovey, and belonged to Gen. McClernand's Corps) with some orders, I suppose, for him to come up. One staff officer after another was dispatched with orders to different commanders, and soon no one was left near my father but myself. Our line was rapidly melting away like snow. Soon a great yell arose from the enemy's line, and they were down upon our men, who began to fall back.

Gen. Grant rode directly forward, and the men recognized him and halted in the cut through which the road passed. The enemy came so near to us that some of their men who were shot fell dead in the road among our own. One of our soldiers, who was about 20 feet in front of us, staggered, but recovering himself turned about, walked up to my father's side, and saluting said, "General, we are giving them h-ll," then fell down exhausted to the ground.

Gen. Grant rode a short distance to the left, apparently much disturbed over the pressure brought upon his soldiers, though showing no excitement; then returning to the right of Hovey's Division, he met the head of Crocker's Division. This division was immediately put into action on Hovey's right; then Logan came up and marched still farther to the right, going around a hill.

We now had 15,000 men in action, making a line nearly three miles long, and the battle raged fiercely from end to end of the line. Very soon the firing becoming heavy on our right, Gen. Grant, with some of the staff, who had now returned to him, rode in that direction.

We first met McPherson, who was mounted on a large black horse, dressed in the full uniform of a Major-General, watching the progress of the fight, which was going on within three hundred yards of where he stood. After stopping for some time with McPherson, we went on to Gen. Logan's command.

As I have said, Logan was called "Fighting Jack Logan" by the men. I do not know that he acquired this soubriquet at Champion's Hill, but surely he deserved it there. He rode a white horse, passing to and fro, dressed in full uniform, exposing himself more than any man in his command while giving directions to each regiment or brigade as he passed it. I believe that could a picture be made of Logan for exhibition as I saw him at Champion's Hill on that bright afternoon, May 16, 1863, every youth and maiden in the land would be his devoted admirer and follower; he was magnificent.

Gen. Grant returned soon to where Hovey was, where, if possible, the battle became heavier. He gave orders to his several staff officers, who went flying in various directions. He then rode to a hill close by, on which we had placed a battery of artillery, where he remained for probably half an hour. The firing became fiercer and fiercer, when suddenly there was heard on the right the hurrah of our men. This shout was taken up by the entire line, and the firing almost ceased. Gen. Grant went to the front of our line, where he found a large number of prisoners, about 3,000, and batteries of artillery occupied nearly every prominent point. I counted 18 guns taken by our men.

We started to ride down the road we had passed over earlier in the day, but found it so covered with dead and wounded men we had to go out to the side, so that our horses should not tramp on them. We rode some little distance, when, seeing a line of skirmishers approaching, Col. Lagow was sent forward to ascertain who they were. Lagow soon returned and reported the line to be the advance of McClernand's Corps. McClernand was too late.

Had he arrived an hour sooner we would probably have captured Gen. Pemberton and his whole army and prevented the necessity of the siege of Vicksburg.[5] We continued our ride toward Edwards's Station, when my father suddenly stopped, turned about, and rode back toward the battlefield. I went into a house close by, which I found filled with Confederate wounded, who had escaped thus far to the rear during the battle. I was greatly fatigued and very hungry, for it was now after sundown and I had not had a mouthful of food or drink since our

---

5 This is unfair since, unless interdicted, a retreating army usually outruns its pursuers. Note also Fred's different attitude toward Sherman, below, who also arrived late; in contrast to Sherman, McClernand was not on good terms with General Grant.

departure from Clinton early that morning; but these wounded men I had come among did not seem to like having a Yankee there, and threatened to kill me.

I wisely left, and soon came upon a picket, who at first seemed more disposed to take me a prisoner than allow me to pass. Some soldier recognized me, however, and I was allowed to go through the lines. All this parleying had attracted the attention of a regiment that was just going into bivouac. They were stacking their guns beside the road, and as I passed some one cried out, "Three cheers for young Grant," which were given with a good will. Thus I was comforted and made happy after my misadventure.

I had not gone far before I reached a house, in front of which I recognized a wagon which belonged to our headquarters.[6] Within this house were Gen. Grant and several of his higher officers, most of whom were greatly elated over their grand victory. Orders were given for the troops to make an early advance the following morning, but according to my recollection my father did not intend to go with them so early. He rested that night upon an old sofa upholstered with carpet, and I slept in the same room with him, finding a comfortable place on the floor.

I was called by my father the next morning [May 17th], who told me I must get ready for the start. My remembrance is that after a light breakfast, taken between 6 and 7 o'clock, we rode off in the direction of the railroad bridge across the Big Black. After rapidly riding for some miles, the troops heartily cheering Gen. Grant as he passed them on the road, we reached the head of the column, commanded by Osterhaus, of McClernand's Corps. All seemed in great confusion, and Gen. Osterhaus, who had been slightly wounded, was with a battery of four 32-pound siege guns, the only heavy ordnance we had, commanded by Maj. Morris Maloney, of the Regular Army.[7] My father rode up to this battery, and after talking with Gen. Osterhaus, who was pale and suffering, he passed on up the road. We halted our horses later at a fine old plantation house, where we dismounted.

Gen. Grant then walked forward to the edge of a woods where there was an old cottonfield, on the opposite side of which we could see the works of the enemy.

The troops were now moved forward to the edge of this cottonfield, and Gen. Grant with his staff returned to the old plantation house. All went upon the porch, except my old friend "Pony" and I. We went off to a pigeon-house we had discovered to find a few squabs, beside doing as we went some other little foraging.

6  Fred and Grant spent the night of 16–17 May at the Isaac Roberts plantation house, which had been Pemberton's headquarters prior to the battle of Champion's Hill.

7  Major Maurice Maloney (See Appendix I) commanded A Company of the regular army's 1st Infantry Regiment, which was equipped with 32-pounder siege guns, in Eugene A. Carr's division of McClernand's corps. *O.R.*, vol. XXI, pt. 2, 151; vol. XXIV, 3, 27.

After getting inside the pigeon-house, I heard a cheer on the right of our line. The enemy opened their artillery upon us, some 17 or 18 guns, and from the number of shots that fell around where I was in the pigeon-house I thought the enemy had determined that I should not have squabs for my supper.[8] I peeped out and found that my comrade, Pony, had retreated in quick order, so that I jumped down and followed back to where my father was, as it was a great comfort to me to be near him. I found him coming down from the house with an officer who was a stranger to me, with whom my father was earnestly conversing.[9]

We all soon mounted our horses and rode to the line of the woods, about half way across the cottonfield, where the troops were in line of battle, moving at a double-quick upon the enemy's line. The firing was not now as brisk as it had been a short time before, and I became enthused, galloped across the field and went over the works within the line of the enemy. There were many Confederates within the works who had surrendered but numbers of them were running, having gone some distance toward the [Big] Black River; there some were crossing near the railroad bridge, which was then on fire, and others made for what was apparently a ferry. I followed these last mentioned, and when I arrived on the bank of the river many were swimming for the opposite shore.

I stopped, and while watching these fellows who were trying to get away some one on the opposite bank fired at me, hitting me in the leg. The wound, though slight, was very painful, and I must have become extremely pale, for just at this time Col. Lagow came dashing up and asked me what had happened to me. I answered that I had been killed, a piece of news, no doubt, surprising to him.[10] He asked where I was hit. I replied in the left leg. He told me to try and move my foot about, which I found I could do very well. He then said: "All right, you are not dead; now let us get away from here quickly."

I returned to the rear with Col. Lagow, having some of my ardor quenched, going as fast as my horse could carry me. When I reached the line of works I found Gens. Grant and McPherson near the prisoners, of whom there were a large number. After a short conversation these two separated, and my father rode to the

---

8 In the 1907 version of his recollections (p. 115), Fred added, "(It is wrong to steal pigeons, anyway.)"

9 The man with Grant was Nathaniel Banks's chief-of-staff, Brig. Gen. William Dwight (see Appendix I), who brought Grant an order dated May 11th from Maj. Gen. Henry Halleck, commanding general of the army in Washington: "If possible, the forces of yourself and of General Banks should be united . . . so as to attack these places [i.e., Vicksburg and Port Hudson] separately with the combined force." Fortunately, as Grant noted, "the order came too late," and he ignored it, despite Dwight's insistence that it was a legitimate order. Grant, *Personal Memoirs*, I:524–526; *O.R.*, XXIV, pt. 1, 36.

10 In the 1907 version, Fred wrote, "Perhaps because I was a boy he presumed to doubt my word." The musket ball nicked Fred's thigh, which would have been painful, but not serious if properly treated.

point from which I had just returned. At this place he decided to have a bridge constructed, which was soon commenced under the direction of Lieut. Hains, who used the house we had occupied as part of the material for the bridge-building. This work continued through the night, and the next morning [May 18th] we crossed the bridge, marching toward Vicksburg.

About half way between the Big Black and Vicksburg we stopped at a house, where my father asked for a drink of water. We were then with the head of the column. The lady of the house came upon the balcony, and seeing that we were Federals and supposing the few troops she then saw to be all our army, said, with contempt: "You Yankees can never take Vicksburg."

To this my father replied: "I expect to do so."

"Why," she said, "it is fortified, and you could not take it in months."

To this father said: "I will capture Vicksburg, if it takes me 30 years."

Just then the solid mass of troops began to come up over the hill and the lady retired, much chagrined.

After a ride of some miles we were joined by Gen. Sherman, who had crossed the Big Black some miles above the railroad bridge, at a small town called Bridgeport. We went on until we were stopped by the firing of the Confederates upon us from their advanced works. As the troops arrived they were sent on to our right and formed in line of battle. When they were all placed in position an advance was ordered by their General, who mounted his horse and rode to Gen. Steele's Division, which was placed at the extreme right. Sherman joined my father, and when we arrived on Walnut Hills, where we could see the Mississippi and Chickasaw Bayou, Gen. Sherman seemed greatly elated and expressed himself with enthusiasm as to the results of this great campaign. When we nearly reached the river some of Steele's men had succeeded in taking an outwork, and were busied in trying to turn it to face the enemy. Several of these outworks were captured before darkness came on, and we went back to where Logan's Division was located and there settled in camp for the night.

Upon the 19th day of May Gen. Grant visited all parts of his command again, spending most of his time with McClernand, who was placed on the left. At this time the number of our troops was not great enough to form a line to reach from the river above to the river below, so that a mere skirmish-line was thrown out to the left. In fact, only a skirmish-line reached to the river south of Vicksburg. I remember that there was considerable anxiety expressed lest Pemberton should make an attack upon our left flank and pass out successfully with his troops.

The 20th and 21st of May were spent in skirmishing and getting our line up as close to the enemy's works as possible, and also in intrenching two important points on our line and building roads in our rear, connecting the different Corps with each other, so that troops could be passed from place to place in case it should become necessary to do so. Upon the morning of the 22d Gen. Grant started with his staff to Gen. Logan's headquarters, which were in front of Fort Hill, on the Jackson road. I think that Fort Hill was considered by my father the strongest and most important point on the Confederate line.[11]

We had stationed at that place a battery of four 32-pound Parrott guns, the only siege artillery I now remember that was in position in front of Vicksburg at the time.[12] Gens. Sherman, McPherson, Logan and Leggett were there, but they soon separated, leaving only Logan with Gen. Grant. These two passed out of the fort to the front, going up a ravine toward the enemy's works. Some of the staff started to go with them, but Gen. Grant bade them all return except Col. Lagow and one of the Orderlies. The four were soon out of sight, and all about was quiet for a few moments.

Suddenly there was a flash of light, then the smoke arose from a cannon in Fort Hill, and we could plainly see that the shot had been fired straight down the ravine that my father and Gen. Logan had entered. Great anxiety and apprehension were expressed by all the staff officers. After some moments, however, Gen. Grant and Logan were seen returning to our lines, their clothing with yellow dirt, thrown over them by the explosion of the shell which we had just seen fired.

After the Generals returned one of our 32-pound guns was fired at the enemy's works, followed by the firing of all the guns to our right and left, until all the artillery placed from the Mississippi on our right over to the left of McClernand's Corps was engaged. The Confederate cannon from the river above to the river below returned the compliments we sent them. From the position I occupied I could see what will probably never be witnessed again in our country, the larger part of an artillery battle covering a distance of nearly seven miles.

Below the smoke of the artillery could be seen distinctly the serried lines of infantry, for the magnificent Army of the Tennessee was moving on to the assault. The enemy's works now became a sheet of fire as his infantry lined his forts and rifle-pits, raining down leaden hail upon our men. The air seemed filled with exploding shells and musket-balls, while the intrepid Logan passed out of our works toward Fort Hill.

---

11 The Confederate defenses at Vicksburg were very elaborate, the result of two years' development. Admiral Porter compared them favorably to the strongest Russian works at Sevastopol during the Crimean War, which were stormed at great cost on Sept. 8, 1855, writing "I saw the celebrated Malakoff and the Redan two days after they fell into the hands of the allied English and French army and they were nothing in comparison with the defenses of Vicksburg." Porter, *Anecdotes*, 132.

12 Major Maloney's guns, noted above.

Drummer Orion Perseus Howe, 14,
55th Illinois, who was awarded
the Medal of Honor.
*National Archives*

All was going on so well in Logan's front that Gen. Grant started toward the right, soon coming up with McPherson, who was at the time with Ransom's Division. Finding everything here encouraging, Gen. Grant continued on toward the right, meeting Gen. Sherman on the road which leads from Haines's Bluff to Vicksburg. A short distance in front of him was the line of troops, toiling bravely on under a most terrific fire. Our flag at one point near the road was at the base of the Confederate parapet.

Gen. Sherman was directing attention to this fact when a small boy, no larger than I, came running from the front. The blood was streaming from a wound in his leg, but he cried out bravely, "General, our regiment is out of ammunition!"

Gen. Sherman wishing to have something done for the lad, began giving directions for some attention to him, when the little fellow, becoming weak from the loss of blood, looked up and said, "Caliber 58," and as he tottered was seized by two soldiers and carried to the rear. I went up to my father to ask him some question at this moment, and found, to my surprise, that his eyes were suffused with tears of sympathy for the brave boy.[13]

Leaving this point we went on further to the right, and then found that the troops there had not made great progress, and in fact were driven back. Soon however a messenger arrived from McClernand, and it was announced that on our left two forts had been carried. Both Gens. Sherman and McPherson were ordered to renew the assault. Gen. Grant and his staff returned toward the left. It was found that the information that had been received about the two forts was untrue.

---

13 This was 14-year-old drummer Orion Perseus Howe of Company C, 55th Illinois Infantry. On May 19th, despite having been wounded in the thigh while helping recover the wounded, Howe volunteered to secure ammunition for the regiment. Later nicknamed "the pet hero of the war" in the regiment, in 1896 he was awarded the Medal of Honor for his courage that day. In the 1907 version of the memoir Fred mistakenly wrote that Howe had called out "Caliber 56!"

A lunet had been stormed, and Serg't Joseph Griffith, of an Iowa regiment, had succeeded in entering.[14] Griffith was struck on the head and stunned, all the rest of the squad being killed or wounded. The Confederates, who were in the lunet, fired a volley just as Griffith recovered his senses. Before they could reload their muskets Griffith sprang to his feet and cried: "I shall kill the first man who disobeys my orders or hesitates to obey."

Then ordering the Confederates to throw away their arms, he marched them out of their works into our lines. Thus through the courage and quick action of a Sergeant 19 prisoners were captured. Among them was a Lieutenant. For this act of gallantry Gen. Grant sent to Griffith a letter the following day, addressed to Lieut. Griffith.

Immediately Griffith came to headquarters to see my father, and stated that as he had had but few advantages he would greatly prefer to be placed so that he might became educated than to be made an officer in the volunteers. Gen. Grant having in his power appointments to West Point from the Congressional Districts in the South then embraced within his command, bestowed upon Griffith one of these appointments. Griffith graduated in the class of 1867, No. 5, but died soon after leaving the Military Academy.

Following the assaults which occurred on the 22d of May, the results of which were only a large casualty list and a few advanced positions, the army settled down to a regular siege. The troops contented themselves with digging approaches, parallels and mines.[15]

The first mine to be exploded was in Leggett's front [June 25th], but did not give to us any great advantage.[16] The story of how "Old Abe," the negro, was blown from the Confederate fort into our line has been told in the *Personal Memoirs of U. S. Grant*.[17] We witnessed a scene on that occasion that would have been ridiculous had it not been for the sight of the nine poor Confederate soldiers who accompanied "Old Abe" in his marvelous aerial flight. The poor fellows all died

---

14 For "lunet" see Appendix VI, for Sgt. Griffith, Appendix I.

15 See Appendix VI.

16 It was on this occasion that Leggett was seriously wounded, putting him out of service for some months.

17 Grant, *Personal Memoirs*, I:551–552: After the explosion of the mine, "All that were there [in the Confederate lines] were thrown into the air, some of them coming down on our side, still alive. I remember one colored man who had been under ground at work [digging a counter-mine] when the explosion took place, who was thrown to our side. He was not much hurt, but terribly frightened. Some one asked him how high he had gone up. 'Dun no, massa, but t'ink 'bout t'ree mile,' was his reply. General Logan commanded at this point and took this colored man to his quarters, where he did service to the end of the siege." Nothing further can be discovered about this man.

Artist's impression of the fighting in the crater at Fort Hill after the mine explosion of June 25th.
*Library of Congress*

from the effects of the explosion. Reinforcements were now arriving and were placed on our left until the gap was filled up between McClernand's left and the Mississippi River.

After the investment was completed the new arrivals were placed at Haines's Bluff, and extended from there to the Big Black and down that stream. They faced toward the east, and under the command of Gen. Sherman they were expected to oppose Gen. Jos. E. Johnston if the latter should attempt to attack our rear, thus trying to force Gen. Grant to abandon the siege of Vicksburg. As there were continual rumors and reports of Johnston being on his way to attack us, all our men were kept on the alert and intensely interested during the remainder of the siege.

The injury which I had received after the battle of Port Gibson and the wound received during the battle of the Big Black caused my leg to swell up and suppurate to such an extent that Dr. Hewitt, our Surgeon, told me that unless I was very careful he would be obliged to amputate my limb. This decision kept me closely confined to camp for some time, where I constantly saw and was near my father and nearly all of the general officers who served with the Army of the Tennessee in that memorable campaign. I have since taken great satisfaction in this, and recall with devotion and great pleasure the officers of that gallant army and many of their characteristics which I grew to know and understand.

My father, who always pursued the even tenor of his way in war as well as in peace, fulfilled each of his duties with method and care. It was a surprise to me even then, mere boy as I was, to see my father quiet and self-possessed when others seemed to be laboring under great excitement. I frequently noticed, however, an intense flashing of his eyes (which were always a clear blue) and a determined expression in his face. On the battlefield Gen. Grant would ride with head erect from one point to another on his line where the heaviest firing was heard, and though quiet in his movements he seemed to take into account everything—the very smallest and seemingly unimportant details. He gave close attention to all that occurred about him, directing his officers and troops with prompt decision.

I remember distinctly that at the battle of Champion's Hill, when he gave to Gen. Logan orders to storm the enemy's line, which move resulted in the capture of 3,000 prisoners and all the Confederate artillery, he turned and almost in the same breath with that he ordered one of his escort to dismount and give a drink of water to a poor wounded soldier near by.

On this campaign he was on horseback during the days, and then late into the night he would be writing his orders, which were long and full of the minutest details. He seemed always the last to retire to rest and the first to rise in the morning. My father possessed, fortunately, an iron constitution, always sleeping well.[18] He always had a small appetite. The only little vanity I ever detected in him was when he alluded occasionally to his physical strength and that of all his family. Knowing of this trait in my father, his great fortitude and patience during his last long illness impressed me deeply. He would prefer to suffer intense pain without a complaint rather than distress those around him.

Gen. Grant was always kind and gentle in his words, considering the feelings of the private soldier as he did those of an officer or one of great rank. A slight reprimand from him seemed to have a marvelous effect. Personally he was loved by his soldiers, and many times my youthful heart throbbed with joy as the cheers and hurrahs of enthusiasm would go up when "The Old Man" (as his men affectionately called him) would pass along the line.[19]

My father rode splendidly, and always on a magnificent and rather fiery horse when possible to obtain one. He had said himself he never uttered an oath. I never heard him use an expression that approached coarseness. I have seen him withdraw from company whose conversation seemed to be verging toward vulgarity. Upon one occasion some gentlemen were chatting, and among them my father; when

---

18 Although his health was generally very good during the campaign, Grant was occasionally ill. For example, on June 15, 1863, he wrote Julia "I have continued well except an attack of Dysentery which now has entirely left me." Grant, *Papers*, vol. 8, 376.

19 "The Old Man" has long been a common moniker in the US Army for a senior commander, so it's not surprising to see it here.

one said, "I know an excellent story which would not be proper to tell before ladies." At this point my father said: "Let us then say that it should not be told before gentlemen."[20]

The commander of the fleet, Admiral Porter, came frequently to headquarters. The Admiral was very fine-looking, and though not large, was a most powerful and well-built man. His forehead was high, his eyes bright, and he had black hair and beard. I recollect that my father seemed to think very highly of Admiral Porter, and was ever ready to sound the praise of this great man. The Admiral handled his fleet with consummate skill, and was always ready to co-operate with the commanders of the army. All concede that Admiral Porter is one of the greatest naval commanders who have ever lived. When the Admiral would come to headquarters he would ride there with several of his staff on horseback. Everyone would then turn out to see "the navy on horseback," as our cavalry escort called them.

On one occasion Admiral Porter came to Gen. Grant's headquarters riding a handsomer horse than usual. Col. Rawlins having asked some questions about his mount, Admiral Porter became enthusiastic over the horse, and describing his good qualities said:

"Do you know, Colonel, that this horse will go just as slowly as one could wish him to."[21]

Although such a great Admiral, Porter's cavalry qualifications might not have quite come up to Gen. P. H. Sheridan's standard.

---

20 Grant's mildness of speech was widely remarked upon at the time and by many historians and biographers since. During the Wilderness campaign, his officers were very surprised when he several times said "Confound it!" or "Doggone it!" or "Darn!" See, for example, Dana, *Recollections of the Civil War*, 43–44; Horace Porter, *Campaigning with Grant: Conversations and Unpublished Letters* (New York, 1897), 164; M. J. Cramer, *Ulysses S. Grant: Conversations and Unpublished Letters* (New York, 1897), 202, quoting John Logan; Edward Longacre, *General Ulysses S. Grant, the Soldier and the Man* (Philadelphia, 2006), 12; Ronald C. White, *American Ulysses: A Life of Ulysses S. Grant* (New York, 2017), 139, 357; Ron Chernow, *Grant* (New York, 2017), 31, 259, 319.

21 Those who knew Porter would likely have considered this a joke on himself, as he was rather fond of horses. In his amusing *Anecdotes and Incidents of the Civil War*, he wrote "My weakness was for horses; I always required a horse. I was in the saddle all the spare time I could find; I did a good deal of business in the saddle, besides keeping myself in health," and "I had quite a stud of horses on board the flagship, and they were indispensable at times for sending messages to army headquarters, etc.," as well as for making the occasional "horse-marine excursion" ashore to hobnob with the generals or pick up some prize. His flagships were usually fitted with a stable and a special gangway that allowed him to mount up aboard ship and ride ashore. Porter, *Anecdotes*, 172, 208, 222, 290.

# Part IV

# Grant's Lieutenants, Corps and Division Leaders of the Invincible Army

## THE STRONGHOLD FALLS, THE WHITE FLAG RAISED AFTER A SIEGE OF 47 DAYS[1]

Gen. McClernand, who commanded the Thirteenth Corps, which during this campaign formed the right wing of the Union army and during the siege formed its left wing, was a very peculiar man. He was as gallant and as brave as an officer could be. He was very ambitious, but having had no training as a soldier, he was not conversant with the duties required of one. He was too proud to ask information of others, and so was never learned in the art of war. I have heard Gov. Oglesby, of Illinois, tell a good anecdote which well illustrates McClernand's lack of knowledge in military matters. It ran as follows: "When Gen. Grant was made a Brigadier-General he was sent to command the District of Southeast Missouri. One of the sub-districts was composed of Cairo and Mound City, Ill. At Cairo were the headquarters of both the district and the sub-district. McClernand had been sent some time before to Cairo to command the sub-district. When Gen. Grant reached there he went immediately to the headquarters and found Oglesby, then Colonel, in command there. He said to Col. Oglesby: "Who is in command here?"

Col. Oglesby replied, " I am, sir."

Then Gen. Grant asked if Gen. McClernand had not yet arrived, and was answered by Oglesby: "Oh, yes, he reached here about three days ago."

"Then," said Gen. Grant, " why is he not in command?"

---

1 Originally published as Fred D. Grant, "General Ulysses S. Grant: His Son's Memories of Him in the Field. Grant's Lieutenants, Corps and Division Leaders of the Invincible Army. The Stronghold Falls; The White Flag Raised After a Siege of 47 Days," *National Tribune*, Feb. 10, 1887, 1.

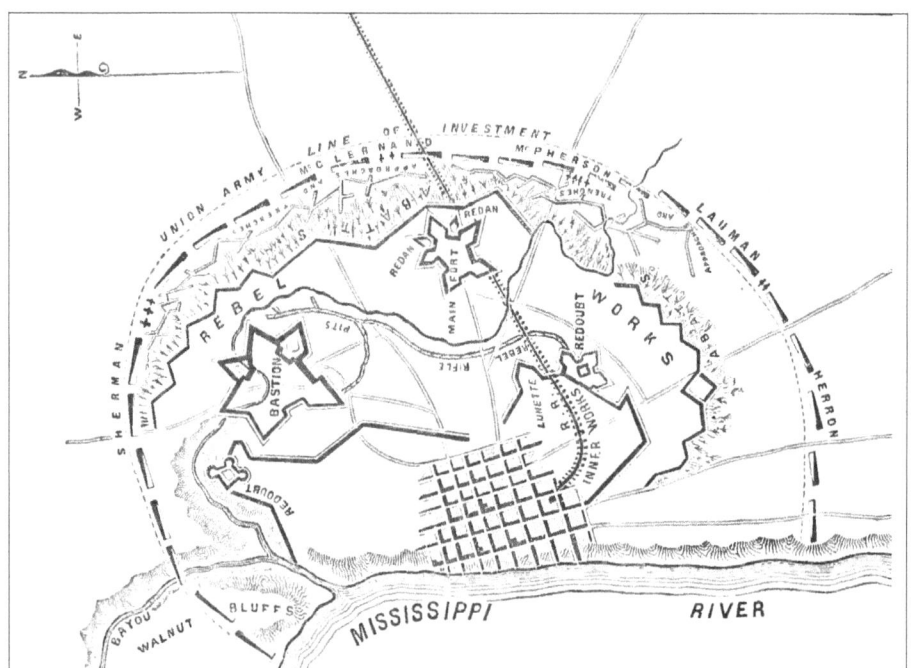

The Vicksburg defenses and siege lines.
*Benjamin F. Gue, History of Iowa from the Earliest Times to the Twentieth Century, Vol. 2*

The Colonel replied, smiling, "I do not know why, unless it is that he does not really know how to assume command."

Gen. Sherman commanded the Fifteenth Corps during part of the siege of Vicksburg, and the remainder of the time he commanded the troops placed back from Haines's Bluff to the Big Black River. He was generally called "Uncle Billy Sherman" by the soldiers. It is useless to try to describe his fine warrior face, so well known to every American. He was regarded by Gen. Grant as his mainstay and support. He was impetuous in action, brilliant in conversation, thoroughly versed in the art of war, but always subordinate, not only willing, but ever holding himself in readiness to obey any order he might receive. It was not necessary for him to have two or three days to prepare for the starting of his corps after the order was given to move. Two hours was more than sufficient for him.

On the 15th of May Gen. Sherman was in Jackson, Miss., attending to affairs there. That night Gen. Grant heard from McPherson, and wishing to have Gen. Sherman at the front, he sent an order for him to move forward. During the afternoon of the 16th of May Gen. Sherman, with the head of his corps, arrived at Bolton, having marched a distance of between 25 and 30 miles that day; and he would have been in the battle of Champion's Hill had the enemy remained upon the field a very short time longer. My father always spoke of Gen. Sherman, as he ever did of Gen. Sheridan, as being one of the most brilliant officers.

Gen. Grant seemed really to feel and express more pleasure when Gen. Sherman received a promotion or any honor than when receiving himself some recognition of his own services. My father not only appreciated the great qualities of Sherman as a soldier, but seemed to have for him the deep and warmest feelings of friendship. It was my own privilege to be with Gen. Sherman on the battlefield under fire, several times, and I, like the troops with him, was inspired with great enthusiasm. I have inherited my father's admiration for this great man.

The next officer in rank, the commander of the Seventeenth Corps, was Maj. Gen. J. B. McPherson, the "Bayard"[2] of the Army of the Tennessee. He was young and very handsome, always splendidly dressed, and mounted on horseback he seemed the picture of the knight he was. McPherson, beloved by his troops and by Gen. Grant, the latter always bestowing upon him a fatherly affection, seemed destined to have a brilliant future. My father's face would brighten with pleasure when listening to McPherson's talk. This officer was most courtly in manner, and the cheers that go up always from the Association of the Army of the Tennessee when this former comrade is mentioned at any of their meetings show with what love and devotion his memory is cherished among them still.

It is said that when Gen. McPherson confronted the enemy at Atlanta and was ordered to surrender, he courteously lifted his hat, bowed low, wheeled his horse about and dashed into the woods before his foe. The Confederates fired a volley at him and he fell instantly dead, brave, courteous and loyal to the last, a great loss to his country, leaving many friends to mourn his untimely end.

Gen. Grant regarded McPherson, from the time the young soldier joined him first at Fort Donelson, as the most promising officer of his age in the army, and he said that in the death of McPherson he had lost one of his best friends and the country one of its ablest defenders. Gen. McPherson, always kind and gentle, made a great pet of me. I was deeply grieved over his death.

Among the division commanders were Gens. Logan, Steele, John E. Smith, Crocker, A. J. Smith, Tuttle, Osterhaus, Blair, Ransom, and Hovey. Besides there were many others whose names are known and whose memories are honored for their courageous services in defense of their country. All of those named I have been fortunate enough to see upon the field of battle. I have heard my father

---

2 The reference is to Pierre Terrail, seigneur de Bayard (c. 1476–1524), usually called the Chevalier de Bayard, known as "*le chevalier sans peur et sans reproche*" (the knight without fear and beyond reproach), a famous French man-at-arms in the waning days of the Age of Chivalry, who was killed in action by musket fire during the Italian Wars (1494–1559). It was an ironic death, given that he executed musketeers as being unchivalrous.

say that "with such officers as these an army must be irresistible." I have before mentioned the enthusiasm felt for Gen. Logan and the admiration always aroused by his magnificent presence and personal courage.

It was claimed by Gen. Logan's enemies that he murdered his foes on the field of battle, crushing them down, utterly annihilating them, a statement of more force and truth than that made against him by his enemies who upon the field of political strife have vented themselves in the silly slander that he murdered his English.[3] Reference to his contests with opponents in the Senate would quickly do away with this ridiculous statement. As the son of my father I was permitted by Gen. Logan to accompany him several times upon the battlefield, and I am proud to say that even then I appreciated in a measure his great qualities as a soldier and many of his valorous deeds and achievements. I was not honored in being so near all the other division commanders, but I saw and realized something of their great services, which are now recorded in the history of the country which they so gallantly defended.

After the assaults of the 22d day of May the siege was continued, without any great excitement being caused, except when occasional reports came in that the Confederates, under Johnston were about to make an attack on our rear. In one of these reports there was enough apparent truth to cause Gen. Grant to make a tour of his line as far as Haines's Bluff, thence back to the Big Black River. He found everything, under the able direction of Gen. Sherman, in readiness to repel any attack from the east, and he returned to his own headquarters camp, just back of Vicksburg.

It was during this tour and at Haines's Bluff that we found some officers recruiting negroes (then called Contrabands) for the new regiments then being raised. I was with one of the recruiting officers, who, approaching a splendid specimen of the African race asked him if he would like to enlist in his company. The darky took off his hat, rubbed his head, shuffled from one foot to the other, pointing to Gen. Grant and staff, answered: "Som' oh dem oder Gen'als wants me, and wid dem all arter me it's hard to tell which comp'ny to jine."

Ajd't-Gen. L. Thomas had been raising colored troops during the campaign, and large numbers had been stationed at Milliken's Bend at the time the army was making the campaign from Bruinsburg to Vicksburg. One day news was received that the enemy had made an attack upon Milliken's Bend and had been repelled by the colored troops.[4] I remember the glee of Col. Rawlins as he read aloud this

3  Fred is here apparently referring to criticisms of Logan's supposed poor use of English by his political foes.

4  Battle of Milliken's Bend (June 6–7, 1863). In an effort to relieve pressure on Vicksburg, Confederate forces west of the Mississippi made a series of attacks on Union posts along the river. On

Artist's impression of the Union siege lines at Vicksburg; it's unlikely the trees would have been undamaged.
*Library of Congress*

message, after finishing which he dropped his hand and said, "And the colored troops fought nobly," a phrase often repeated later in the war.[5] This was the first engagement of any consequence fought by the colored troops, and had a very good

June 6th at Milliken's Bend, some 1,500 Confederates attacked the Union garrison, which totaled 1,100–1,200 troops, consisting of some 120–160 white veterans from the 23rd Iowa, and the rest African American recruits, most virtually untrained, under White officers in the 9th Louisiana Native Guards (later the 63rd US Colored Infantry), 11th (49th USCI) and 13th Louisiana Infantry, African Descent (which never completed training), and the 1st Mississippi, African Descent (51st USCI). The Confederates drove the defenders into the earthworks by nightfall, but then paused to rest and prepare for a night attack. At about 3:00 a.m. on the 7th, they resumed their attack, reportedly to cries of "No Quarter!" Fighting was fierce, quickly coming to hand-to-hand, and lasted some nine hours, when the defenders, supported by fire from two newly arrived gunboats, counterattacked with the bayonet, driving off the Confederates. Casualties are uncertain. Estimated Confederate losses range from about 450 (150 killed and 300 wounded) to 186 total. Those for the 23rd Iowa are given as 23 killed and 43 wounded, while those for the African American regiments range greatly, with the lower estimates more likely: 96 to 127 officers and men killed, 200 to 280 wounded, and between 132 and 300 missing, many of whom were never found and are believed to have been murdered or carried off into servitude in Texas. See Geo. W. Williams, *A History of the Negro Troops in the War of the Rebellion, 1861–1865* (New York, 1888), 224–228, and particularly Linda Barnickel, *Milliken's Bend: A Civil War Battle in History and in Memory* (Baton Rouge, 2013). Among the murdered prisoners were two White officers, Capt. Corydon Heath (9th Louisiana Infantry, African Descent) and 2nd Lt. George L. Conn (4th Louisiana Infantry, African Descent). *Official Army Register of the Volunteer Force of the United States Army for the Years 1861, '62, '63, '64, '65*, vol. 8 (Washington, D.C., 1867), 152, 222.

5  Fred's comment about the recurrence of the phrase "And the colored troops fought nobly" was true. It appeared often in newspaper and other accounts during and after the war about African American troops, but was also used ironically in racist accounts of Black criminals or victims of White rioters. The phrase was so popular the German American painter Louis Schultze (1820–1900) executed a work bearing it as a title, exhibited at the National Academy of Design in 1867. It has unfortunately since been lost. Schultze's most well-known work is probably a portrait of Dred Scott,

effect upon the army, inasmuch as it proved that the negroes would fight and help to liberate themselves.[6]

Throughout the entire siege many interesting incidents occurred, which have, however, (many of them) been often told; but one event took place that gave rise to much talk among the soldiers, and this I may repeat here. It excited interest in me at the time of the occurrence.

After the army had arrived in the immediate rear of Vicksburg, many visitors came from the North, hoping to see their friends and relatives in the army. About this time I was one day on the skirmish-line where the 8th Mo. was stationed, and being attracted by a group of soldiers near an advanced point, all talking and showing some excitement, I hastened toward them with a boy's natural curiosity to investigate matters, and found that one of our visitors from the North had expressed the desire to have a bullet-hole put through his hat, to carry home with him as a souvenir, or specimen of shot from our enemy's guns. The boys of the 8th Mo., being willing and eager to accommodate him, took the gentleman to that part of the field where I now found them assembled, and bade him hold his hat high above the works, saying the Johnnies would fix it all right for him. He did as they directed, but not thinking to put a stick or ramrod under his hat, as he should have done, the bullet penetrated not only his hat but his hand; bringing to this ambitious civilian some pain, as well as glory, to carry home. The boys of the 8th regiment were filled with regret over the accident, but consoled themselves with the thought that the gentleman would go back to the North quite "satisfied with his scars."[7]

Every day during the siege the paper that was printed in the city of Vicksburg was sent to Gen. Grant, who receiving it, fully realized that there must be constant communication existing between the armies. An effort was made to find out what and where this line of communication was. It was discovered that there were some

---

held by the Missouri Historical Society. "Louis Schultze," *askART* website, https://www.askart.com/artist/Louis_Schultze/89333/Louis_Schultze.aspx, accessed Aug. 22, 2021.

6  When these memoirs were republished as "Fred Grant as a Boy with the Army" in *Confederate Veteran* XVI, no. 1 (Jan. 1908), 10–14, his comments on African American troops ended with the quote from the African American potential recruit, thus omitting mention of Black valor at Milliken's Bend and the role of African-American troops in their own liberation.

7  If Fred's identification of the regiment is correct, he is referring to the 8th Missouri, "The American Zouaves," which was composed mostly of Irish Americans or recent Irish immigrants. It mustered into service in June 1861, and took part in most of the major actions in the Western theater: Fort Donelson, Shiloh, Corinth, Fort Hindman, Yazoo Pass, the Vicksburg campaign, Chattanooga, Missionary Ridge, the Atlanta campaign, and Sherman's March to the Sea. After the latter many veterans were discharged, but a remnant of the regiment fought at Bentonville in March 1865. The regiment lost 81 officers and enlisted men to combat, and 125 to disease; eight men received the Medal of Honor.

Missourians in the Confederate lines, and that they were in the habit of carrying out communication with their friends of the 7th and 8th Mo. of our side.[8] They evidently carried on a little trade, our men giving various articles of food for tobacco and learning as much news as they could of what was going on in the city. At first some of this traffic was broken up, but ere long the intercourse was winked at, as the information contained in this way was found to be so valuable and important. I presume that Pemberton learned as much about us and our movements as we did of him and his troops.

Once during the siege, while out on the line with Gen. A. J. Smith, a flag of truce appeared, which Gen. Smith advanced to receive, taking with him Col. Lagow and myself.[9] The Confederate officers thus received were Gen. Bowen and Col. Montgomery (I think of Pemberton's staff) and another officer.[10] The guns on Smith's immediate front ceased to fire, but the rest of the line, including the fleet, continued to throw shells into the city. Gen. Smith or Col. Lagow proposed to have this firing stopped, when Col. Montgomery spoke up, saying: "Do not trouble yourselves, gentlemen; it really does no harm."

When asked if our artillery had not done great damage in the city of Vicksburg, he replied: "Yes; last week you actually killed a cow."

It was proved when the city was surrendered that Col. Montgomery must have been guilty of boasting. I did not know, or have forgotten, why Col. Montgomery was sent over the lines, or what his mission was.

Our parallels were slowly approaching Vicksburg now. Many deserters were coming into our lines, reporting that their garrison was in a most desperate condition. Rumors came in to us that Johnston had left Jackson, to attack our rear and thus raise the siege. These numerous rumors caused great anxiety among the soldiers and younger officers about my father's headquarters, and in some way a firm belief gained credence that an assault was contemplated by our command, and that the city of Vicksburg was to be carried by storm on the 1st of July. I

8 There were Missourians in both armies. Grant had 19 regiments of Missouri infantry and one of cavalry, plus seven artillery companies, while Pemberton had eight regiments of Missouri infantry or dismounted cavalry, and five artillery companies.

9 Apparently the flag of truce was initially not properly displayed, and the two men were under fire until Lt. Col. Montgomery (see Appendix I), realized his error. Winston Groom, *Vicksburg, 1863* (New York, 2009), 410–411; Napier Bartlett, *A Soldier's Story of the War: Including the Marches and Battles of the Washington Artillery and of Other Louisiana Troops* (New Orleans, 1873), 13, 115.

10 According to Grant (*Personal Memoirs*, I:556), there were only two officers, Bowen and Montgomery. Fred may have mistaken an escorting Union officer for a Confederate.

presume this rumor was carried into the Confederate lines, for on the 3rd of July a report was brought in of a flag of truce.[11]

I was with my father when this news reached him, but I noticed no excitement in his manner while receiving it. Later in the afternoon of the same day Gen. Grant took with him several of his staff and rode out to our line fronting Fort Hill, I accompanying them. Here most of the officers dismounted and General Grant was joined by Gens. Logan, McPherson, A. J. Smith and several others, all distinguished men. In a short time a white flag was seen floating over the enemy's works.

All firing ceased on that part of the lines nearest us, and a party of Confederates were seen passing out of their fortifications. Gen. Grant and his officers left our works and walked up the side of the hill, meeting under an old tree the Confederates, Gen. Pemberton, Gen. Bowen, Col. Montgomery, and one or two others.[12]

Gen. Grant saluted Gen. Pemberton most pleasantly, and after some general conversation the assembled officers soon broke up into three parties. Gens. Grant and Pemberton went to one side, talking to each other with interest. Then Gens. McPherson, A. J. Smith, Logan and Brown formed another party, passing over some distance on the right of the first party. The remaining number of officers staid [sic] where first assembled, where they conversed with each other. Looking up, I beheld the works on both sides lined with the brave soldiers.

This was the first time since the 18th of May that any man of either of the two great armies could have been exposed to view without being immediately fired upon by the other side. Ere long Gen. Grant arose from a comfortable seat he had found upon the ground and came over to the tree where our party was collected. He was quickly joined by McPherson, and soon all, including Bowen's party, left,

---

11 Fred's lack of comment about the progress of the siege following the attacks in late May through the eve of the surrender was probably due to ill health. His wound had become infected, and he was suffering from several diseases, which caused him to miss much of the siege. During this period he spent most of his time in his father's company or with family. Toward the end of May, he was sent to recuperate with his mother's sister, Emma Dent Casey, in Caseyville, Kentucky. While there, he celebrated his 13th birthday (May 30). Within days, however, Confederate irregulars learned of his presence and attempted to capture him but were diverted by Mrs. Casey. That brave woman promptly put him on a steamboat to Cairo, and he returned to his father's side. On June 9th, the general reassured his wife that "Fred. has enjoyed his campaign very much. He has kept a journal." His health remaining poor, Grant sent him to stay with his Uncle Lewis in St. Louis, writing Julia on June 15th: "Fred has been complaining a little for a few days. His Uncle Lewis was down this morning and I let him go back with him to spend a short time. I have proposed to Fred. to go to St. Louis several times but he objects. He wants to see the end of Vicksburg." On the 29th, Grant wrote Julia: "Fred. has returned from his uncles. He does not look very well but is not willing to go back until Vicksburg falls." Grant, *Papers*, vol. 8, 332, 376–377, 444–445. See also Farina, *Ulysses S. Grant*, 208.

12 There was some irony in the meeting between Grant and Pemberton: They had served together during the Mexican War. At the war's end, General Winfield Scott had written a commendation for Grant which was delivered to him by Pemberton.

U. S. Grant and John C. Pemberton, negotiating surrender terms on July 3, 1863.
*Harper's Weekly*

after this short consultation, Gen. Grant and officers returning to the Union lines, and the Confederates passing to their own fortifications.

Upon his return to headquarters my father was joined by several prominent Generals, and many others in command were added to the party soon afterward. The largest assemblage of General officers which it had been my good fortune to see at any one time were on that memorable afternoon crowded around an entrance to a little tent seven by nine feet large. Here sat or stood in converse the great heroes of the most brilliant campaign and siege that is recorded in the history of the world, deciding upon and settling the fate of their foes. They had conquered and taken in their power the largest number of men, the greatest quantity of war materials and spoils ever surrendered in battle.[13]

Here was Gen. McPherson beaming with pleasure over the triumph. Here was the gray-haired, reliable, faithful old soldier, E. O. C. Ord. I saw Logan here, no

13 Although by no means the greatest operation in military history, Fred's evident pride in his father's accomplishment is certainly understandable, as Vicksburg is widely considered by scholars and military professionals as one of the most brilliant operations in U.S. military history.

longer fierce and stormy, but with countenance wreathed in smiles, as he fastened about his fine figure more securely the sash and sword-belt he wore. Near Logan was the gallant Fred. Steele, who afterward did such grand service in the Trans-Mississippi Department. Here there were many other brave and loyal officers who had won for themselves rank, and won the constellation upon their shoulders upon many bloody but glorious battlefields from the Ohio River to Vicksburg.

After much conversation, in which all took cheerful part, Gen. Grant turned, sat down at his little pine table and wrote a message which was dispatched at once to one of our outposts to be forwarded to the commander of the brave defenders of the garrison. Then the assembled officers separated and scattered, most of them going to the tents of the various staff officers. As I then occupied the same tent with my father I went into it after the consultation was over, and remained sitting for some time upon a little bed made of cane, which the soldiers had built for me. I felt restless and knew not what I was waiting for, while my father sat busily writing.

Just then a messenger was announced, and being brought in he handed to Gen. Grant a note, which he opened immediately. In a moment my father gave a sigh of relief and said calmly, "Vicksburg has surrendered!" a great piece of news, though not surprising. In this way I happened to be the first to hear that the Gibraltar of America had been forced to fall before the Army of the Tennessee.

Upon the announcement of Vicksburg's surrender I felt enthused, going rapidly from my father's tent to tell the news to my kind friends of the cavalry escort. Officers were hurrying to and fro, and when I returned in the direction of Gen. Grant's quarters I saw there, clustered about, the happiest assemblage of veterans and warriors that the mind could picture. They did not fully realize then the real grandeur of their own victory even; they did know, however, that from that time on the Mississippi would "flow unvexed to the sea."[14]

Upon the following morning, July 4, after partaking of an early breakfast, and the horses all being in readiness, Gen. Grant with his staff rode to the front upon the Jackson road.

I recollect that before the starting of the officers many guns were heard. From the reports of them it seemed that those on our right were engaged in the firing, and Gen. Grant expressed great surprise at this, and remarked: "Steele should know better than to allow that."

He even went so far as to say, I believe, that he "should be arrested," when just then Steele rode up and asked where we thought the firing was. Gen.

---

14 Fred is here referring to Lincoln's comment, upon learning of the surrender of Vicksburg, "Thank God, The Father of Waters again goes unvexed to the sea."

Grant responded: "I was about to order your arrest, Steele, on account of that sounding of guns."

When this officer explained all, and said that he thought that the reports came from Laumann's front, a messenger was immediately sent to have the firing stopped. Gen. Grant took no delight in triumphing over the vanquished.

After the front of our army was reached, we could see the white flags floating over the lines of the parapets of the enemy. Soon after Confederate troops began to file in order out of their works and stack their firearms between the two lines of the armies. It was a wonderful sight. Thirty-one thousand six hundred brave men, with 172 cannon, laying down 60,000 muskets at the feet of this conquering Army of the Tennessee, their brave but lenient foes.

The arms being stacked with care outside, the garrison marched back into the works. Then Gen. Grant started forward at the head of his troops, Gen. Logan's Division leading, to take formal possession of the city. As our army passed over the works, great admiration was expressed by our officers at the splendid forts of the enemy, which had kept our army from entering the city for 47 days.

Gen. Grant passed on until he reached a house of some pretentious appearance, partially built of stone.[15] There was an assemblage of Confederate officers upon the porch. Gen. Grant dismounted at this place and entered. No one met him at the gate or asked him to take a seat among them. Gen. Pemberton was there, with his staff, but he received his conqueror in a most frigid, cold manner. After a moment Gen. Grant said: "I would like a drink of water; where can I find it?"

One young officer more politely inclined than others, pointed to the door of the house, and said: "I presume you will find a glass of water inside the house."

Gen. Grant went back through the house and entered the kitchen. I followed him. There was an old negress, who gave us the coveted drink. Perhaps our enemies there assembled did not realize that that same morning my father had interfered with any firing or saluting in exultation over the victory. Some of the others of their army later in the war appreciated deeply the clemency and justice ever shown them by Gen. Grant in moments of his greatest victories.

The staff who accompanied him that morning felt indignant over the manner of his reception. Gen. Grant, however, felt satisfied in capturing Vicksburg, but had only sympathy and considerate kindness at heart for the conquered; and they knew him better later on in the frightful struggle between the North and the South, and many times officers taken by the enemy would find warm and cordial greetings awaiting them among foes who had perhaps in the past been classmates or friends.

---

15  This house does not seem to have been identified. It was not that of planter and merchant William Samuel Lum, in which Grant set up his headquarters the following day; see below.

After getting a glass of water, Gen. Grant returned to the balcony and conversed for some time with Gen. Pemberton, and then rode on into the city of Vicksburg. The Union flag had been placed upon the courthouse by Gen. Logan's troops.

My father, after passing through the principal parts of the city, went on to the river, where he found most of the naval vessels had arrived, and boarded the *Benton*. Admiral Porter cordially congratulated Gen. Grant upon his great victory. My father seemed extremely quiet and thoughtful, though satisfied and pleased with his success. He never seemed to show the enthusiastic exultation so common at such a time as this.

The sad depression of his enemies affected him, and he did not dwell upon his victory greater than any other recorded in the annals of history. Gen. Grant moved with his staff into Vicksburg upon the next day, July 5, occupying as his quarters the house of a pleasant old gentleman named Lum, who at first disliked to meet my father, but who afterward became his warm friend, and showed always affectionate remembrance of my father's conduct toward him and his family at that time.[16] Some of the most beautiful letters received during Gen. Grant's last illness were from this family of Mr. Lum.

By the time of the capture of Vicksburg I had become so weak from an illness produced by exposure in my army life, that I was sent home to the North upon the 8th of July, and was unfortunately destined not to be able to rejoin my father until after the battle of Chattanooga.[17]

In sending at your request the foregoing lines, Mr. Editor, I have given an account of the campaign and siege of Vicksburg just as I then saw it all when a mere lad less than 13 years of age. I have refrained from reference to data, relying entirely upon my memory in relating the events which then passed before me.

---

16 Planter and merchant William Samuel Lum (1822–1899) and his wife Mary Aseneth Griffin Lum (1823–1870), had assets of some $38,000, including 48 enslaved people. "William S. Lum," US Census 1860 and "William S. Lum," U.S. Census 1860, Slave Schedule. On July 5, 1863, Grant took up residence on the first floor of the Lum's three story, 26-room mansion overlooking the Mississippi, quarters formerly occupied by Pemberton. Julia and the children soon joined him. The Lums and their six children were initially somewhat cold, but soon became friendlier toward their guests, Lum's widowed mother Anna Maria Owings Lum (1796–1870) proving a gracious hostess. Fred became quite friendly with one of the Lum's daughters, most likely Mary Lina (1849–1940), even allowing her to ride his pony, perhaps his first "crush." The children's governess, 23-year-old Connecticut native Mary Emeline "Emma" Hurlbut (1840–1874), was courted by some of Grant's staff officers, and later that year married his chief-of-staff, Col. John A. Rawlins. Julia Grant, *Personal Memoirs*, 120ff; Rebecca Blackwell Drake, "Union Headquarters: The Lum House: Recollections of Vicksburg from The Personal Memoirs of Julia Dent Grant," Battle of Raymond website, http://battleofraymond. org/history/lum.htm, accessed Aug. 23, 2021; Carter III, *The Final Fortress*, 310. Sometime after the Grants left Vicksburg, the Lum house was demolished, supposedly as an act of "random violence" on Sherman's orders.

17 See "Fred Grant's War After Vicksburg" on page 76.

If in contributing my story I furnish the least amusement to any of my father's brave comrades of that time, I am more than amply repaid. In seeing so much of all that transpired during our war I owe my good fortune not only to the indulgence and kindness of my father, but also to the intercession of my mother, who was anxious to have me realize the important events that were then occurring, and thought of what my future gratitude would be at having followed my father during his army career.

Gen. Grant was never too anxious or too much engrossed in his affairs of great importance to neglect showing thoughtfulness and consideration to those about him. Thus my life in camp was always happy. I remember with affection many of the actors in the great drama of 1861–'65. I passed much of my time with the private soldiers, who were ever kind to me. For many of the most agreeable memories of the war I now have I owe to "the boys," who were never too tired or worn out to comfort or "pet" the son of "The Old Man." This name for my father was used by many of his officers as well as soldiers. I am grateful for my association with them all, and almost claim the rank of "veteran."[18]

18 Fred is mentioned as a veteran on several monuments erected by the veterans of the Army of the Tennessee, despite the fact that he was not actually in the army. In remarks at the reunion of the veterans of the Army of the Tennessee, William T. Sherman, society president, observed "Colonel Fred Grant is fully entitled to membership here, for he was with us at Vicksburg," *Proceedings of the Eighteenth Meeting of the Society of the Army of the Tennessee* (Cincinnati, 1893), 194; see also, for example, "Grant, Frederick D.," Wisconsin Veterans' Museum, https://wisvetsmuseum.pastperfectonline.com/byperson?keyword=Grant%2C+Frederick+D, accessed Oct. 1, 2021.

# Section II

# Fred Grant, in Context

## THE GRANT FAMILY AND THE CIVIL WAR

The Grants arrived in Massachusetts from England in 1630, to take up farming in Connecticut. During the French and Indian War (1756–1763), U. S. Grant's great-grandfather, Noah Grant II (1718–1756) served in Roger's Rangers, rising to the rank of captain, and commanding a company that included some African American soldiers.[1] On September 20, 1756, Captain Grant disappeared while scouting near Ft. William Henry, close by Lake George, New York, and was presumed to have been killed by Indians. A Grant family tradition has it that the president's grandfather, Noah III (1748–1819), took part in the "Boston Tea Party." He certainly served in the Revolutionary War, fighting his way from Bunker Hill to Yorktown, also rising to captain. After the Revolution, this Captain Grant took his family to the Ohio country to farm the land granted to him as a veteran. Several of U. S. Grant's uncles served in the War of 1812, but his father, Jesse Grant (1794–1873) did not.[2]

The man now known as Ulysses S. Grant, was born Hiram Ulysses Grant on April 27, 1822. Although not studious, as a young man, "Lyss" received excellent schooling, and, availing himself of the opportunity of a free higher education,

---

1  John Reeves, *Soldier of Destiny: Slavery, Secession, and the Redemption of Ulysses S. Grant* (New York, 2023), 24–25.

2  Ulysses S. Grant Presidential Library, Ulysses S. Grant Genealogy, https://www.usgrantlibrary.org/usgrant/genealogy, accessed Aug. 22, 2022.

entered West Point in 1839. There his name was somehow transmogrified into the more familiar Ulysses S. Grant, the new middle initial standing for his mother's maiden name, Simpson. Grant graduated in 1843, 21st out of a class of 39, fourteen of whom became generals in Blue, and four in Gray. Grant aside, none of them enjoyed unusually distinguished careers. Earning a reputation as a superb horseman, he was commissioned a second lieutenant in the 4th Infantry Regiment.[3]

## U. S. GRANT AND JULIA BOGGS DENT

In the spring of 1844, Brevet Second Lieutenant Ulysses S. Grant met Julia Boggs Dent (January 26, 1826–December 14, 1902), the sister of his former West Point roommate Brevet Second Lieutenant Frederick Dent (December 17, 1820–December 23, 1892), at her family home in Missouri. It was the beginning of one of the great love matches in American history. Within weeks the couple became engaged. But marriage had to be postponed. In part this was because the Dents were slaveholders, and Grant's parents, inclined to abolition, opposed the match. And then the war with Mexico intervened.

Although he had serious reservations about the justice of the war with Mexico (1846–1848), Grant remained in the army and accumulated a distinguished war record. Initially assigned to Zachary Taylor's little army on the Rio Grande, Grant fought in the battles of Palo Alto and Resaca de la Palma in May 1846, and took part in the battle for Monterrey the following September. In one of the early defining events of his military career, he volunteered to carry orders under fire, in a mad-dash horse gallop through town, hanging off the side of his horse, keeping it between himself and the enemy, displaying the conspicuous coolness under fire that characterized his Civil War service. Early in 1847 his regiment was transferred to Winfield Scott's army, and Grant took part in the siege of Vera Cruz in March, the battles of Cerro Gordo (April), Churubusco (August), and Molino del Rey, as well as in the storming of Chapultepec Castle and the final capture of Mexico City (all September). Although for most of this campaign Grant served as regimental quartermaster, he voluntarily took part in several actions and earned two brevet—honorary—promotions and a citation for merit from General Scott, which was delivered to him by 1st Lt. John Pemberton. Grant returned to the United States in April 1848.

---

3 Martin Dugard, *The Training Ground: Grant, Lee, Sherman, and Davis in the Mexican War, 1846–1848* (Lincoln, NE, 2009), 12*ff*; Stephen L. Harris, *Duty, Honor, Privilege* (Washington, D.C., 2001), 30, 36–37, 69.

On August 22, 1848, Grant and Julia were married at her parent's home in St. Louis. Grant's parents did not attend but did welcome Julia into the family. Soon after their marriage, Grant, by then a first lieutenant, was assigned to garrison duty at Detroit, where the Grants began to raise a family. The couple had four children: Frederick Dent Grant (May 30, 1850–April 12, 1912), Ulysses S. Grant, Jr. (July 22, 1852–Sept. 25, 1929), nicknamed "Buck," Ellen Wrenshall Grant (July 4, 1855–Aug. 30, 1922), known as "Nellie," and Jesse Root Grant II (Feb. 6, 1858–June 8, 1934), named after Ulysses's father. From all the evidence, the Grants were a close, very loving family.

In the spring of 1852 Grant's regiment, the 4th Infantry, was ordered to California by way of Panama. Julia, pregnant with their second child, did not accompany him, staying with his family in Ohio. This was fortunate, for during the crossing of the Isthmus of Panama, cholera broke out, and about a seventh of the troops and accompanying wives and children died.

Initially stationed in Oregon, in August of 1853 Grant was promoted to captain and assigned command of a company at the newly established Fort Humboldt, in Eureka, California. The tedious, boring routine of garrison duty and the long absence from his family led Grant to occasional instances of "intemperance." Reprimanded by his commanding officer, Maj. Robert C. Buchanan, Grant promised to reform or resign. A subsequent incident caused him to submit his resignation as of July 31, 1854.

Over the next few years Grant tried his hand at farming some of his father-in-law's land and engaged in several small business ventures, all with limited success. Despite living on the edge of poverty, Grant showed considerable strength of character when, after his father-in-law gave him an enslaved man, Grant freed the fellow, rather than sell him for cash. By the eve of the Civil War Grant was working as a clerk in his father's leather goods business in Galena, Illinois. His prospects seemed dubious.

## THE GRANTS AND THE CIVIL WAR

On the outbreak of the Civil War, U. S. Grant, a Douglas Democrat, immediately threw himself into supporting the Union cause. With the help of his friend Congressman Elihu B. Washburne, Grant secured an appointment as military advisor to Governor Richard Yates of Illinois. By mid-May he had helped raise ten regiments of volunteers at Camp Yates, near Springfield. Although denied reinstatement in the regular army, on June 16th, 1861, Grant was appointed a colonel in the volunteer army and assumed command of the 21st Illinois Volunteers on the 18th. The day before he had written to Julia asking if she would let 11-year-

The Grant family, c. 1865; from left to right, Mrs. Grant, Fred,
standing behind Nellie, the general, Jesse, and U. S. Grant, Jr., "Buck."
*National Park Service, Ulysses S. Grant and Julia Dent Grant Virtual Museum*

old Fred and 9-year-old Buck join him for a month. She agreed to let Fred go.[4] On June 22nd, after a brief visit with his family in Galena, Colonel Grant returned to his regiment at Camp Yates, accompanied by Fred.[5]

Fred would spend nearly three weeks with the regiment, watching his father drill the troops, attending its formal muster into Federal service on June 28th, and then following it as it moved around the state, to Quincy, Allinson's Grove, Naples, Quincy again, and then West Quincy, in Missouri. He appears to have thoroughly enjoyed himself, especially once Grant procured him a horse, and the troops quickly took to him. On July 7th Grant wrote Julia, "The Soldiers and officers call him 'Colonel' and he seems to be quite a favorite."[6]

On July 10th, the regiment was alerted for field service against rumored incursions by Confederate irregulars across the Mississippi into western Illinois. On July 12th, Grant, concerned for Fred's safety, put him on a steamboat at Quincy, bound for Dubuque, where he could catch a train for Galena.[7] The next day, Grant wrote his wife:

> Fred. started home yesterday and I did not telegraph you because I thought you would be in a perfect stew until he arrived. He did not want to go atall and I felt lothe [sic] at sending him but now that we are in the enemies country I thought you would be alarmed if he was with me. Fred. is a good boy and behaved very manly.[8]

Before Fred arrived home, Julia wrote, "Do not send him home; Alexander was not older when he accompanied Philip," a reference to Alexander the Great, who accompanied his father King Philip of Macedon on campaign when he was 16, a bit older than Fred, a comment which appears to have amused her husband.[9]

---

4  Grant, *Papers*, vol. 2, 42.

5  Ibid., 49–50. Although Grant didn't command the 21st Illinois for very long, the regiment had a busy war, seeing action in Missouri, Kentucky, Tennessee, Georgia, and more, not mustering out of service until December of 1865, in Texas. The regiment lost 130 officers and enlisted men in combat and 142 dead of disease.

6  Ibid., 49–50, 53, 59–60.

7  Grant, *Personal Memoirs*, I:248.

8  Grant, *Papers*, vol. 2, 70.

9  Grant, *Personal Memoirs*, I:247–248; Julia Dent Grant, *The Personal Memoirs of Julia Dent Grant* (Mrs. Ulysses S. Grant), ed. John Y. Simon (New York, 1975), 92.

Unbeknownst to both Grant and Julia as they penned their letters, when Fred reached Dubuque, the train had already left. Rather than wait a day for another train, he walked the 18 miles to Galena, arriving tired, but safe.[10]

On August 26th Grant, recently promoted to brigadier general of volunteers, wrote Julia, "I am sorry that I did not keep Fred with me. He would have enjoyed it very much."[11] A month later, on September 29th, while at Cairo, Illinois, Grant wrote "By the way. I would like to take Fred. with me the balance of the Campaign. Wont you let him come? If you will send him down when father comes, I will take good care of him."[12]

Over the next 18 months or so, Fred, his mother, and the other children visited the general from time to time, notably when he was at Cairo, and even paid occasional visits to him in the field. For example, Fred arrived at his father's headquarters at Fort Henry on February 10, 1862, but went home within a day or so, his father later writing "I shall always regret that I did not take Fred. with me to Fort Donelson."[13] Then, on March 5, 1863, having already touched upon the matter earlier, Grant reminded Julia "that I want Fred. to come and stay with me."[14]

Thus began Fred's three months in the field during the Vicksburg campaign.

## FRED GRANT'S WAR AFTER VICKSBURG

Fred was ill during the final weeks of the siege of Vicksburg and spent most of his time at his father's quarters. On June 29th Grant wrote Julia that Fred "does not look very well but is not willing to go back until Vicksburg falls." On July 8th, four days after the surrender, Grant sent Fred to his mother in St. Louis. Fred later told a journalist that he was suffering from dysentery, his weight having fallen from 110 pounds to 68, and that he also had a toothache.[15]

After Fred recovered, he attended school in St. Louis, and did not see his father again until after the battle of Chattanooga, when the general made a brief visit to his

10 Julia Dent Grant, *Personal Memoirs*, 92.

11 Grant, *Papers*, vol. 2, 82, 141.

12 Ibid., 327–328.

13 Ibid., vol. 4, 188, 211, 409.

14 Ibid., 22.

15 Ibid., vol. 8, 444–445; vol. 10, 27, 48; E. Watrous, "Grant as His Son Saw Him: An Interview With Colonel Frederick D. Grant About His Father," *McLure's Magazine* II, no. 6 (May 1894): 517.

family.[16] In early January 1864, while Grant was at Nashville, Fred became gravely ill with "Typhoid Pneumonia." Grant went on leave and spent a few days with Fred, who had begun to recover. The general shortly returned to the army. When Fred was able to travel, he and his mother went to stay with Grant at Nashville.[17] During this period the general was busy planning further operations, notably moves against Mobile and Atlanta, and against James Longstreet's forces in eastern Tennessee. Meanwhile, Congress revived the rank of lieutenant general, vacant since the death of George Washington in 1799. Grant's promotion to lieutenant general was confirmed on March 2, 1864, and he was ordered to Washington the next day. Accompanied by Fred, Grant arrived in Washington on the evening of the 8th, received his commission the following day, and was then given command of the armies of the United States. Fred stayed with his father for more than two weeks, while the general met with Lincoln, Secretary of War Stanton, and others to begin laying plans and discussing assignments for various generals. Fred accompanied his father on visits to the Army of the Potomac and other commands. Shortly after mid-March, Fred returned to his mother in St. Louis.[18]

Over the next months, as Grant planned and conducted the Overland campaign, Fred remained in St. Louis with the rest of the family. On June 20th, with the armies having settled into the lines about Petersburg and Richmond, Grant wrote Julia from City Point, suggesting she come east and stay with Benjamin Butler and his wife. "If you were at Fortress Monroe you could occasionally come to City Point when the Dispatch steamer is coming up and go back with it. I would keep Fred & Buck with me most of the time, and Jess too some times," Grant persuaded his wife.[19] Fred spent a few days with his father at City Point, but his health remaining poor, soon returned to his mother.[20] In late August 1864, Fred, his mother, and his siblings enjoyed a short visit with his father, during

---

16 Fred mentions this visit after Chattanooga in most versions of his memoir. For example see page 68 as well as Frederick Dent Grant, "With Grant at Vicksburg," *The Outlook* 59, no. 9 (July 2, 1898): 543; Frederick D. Grant, "A Boy's Experience at Vicksburg," *Personal Recollections of the War of the Rebellion: Addresses Delivered Before the New York Commandery of the Loyal Legion of the United States*, ed. Alexander Noel Blakeman, James Grant Wilson, and Titus Munson Coan Blakeman (New York, 1907), 100.

17 Grant, *Papers*, vol. 10, 47 note 2; 69, 102, 13, 215–218.

18 Ibid., 226. Fred's younger brother Jess, just six, joined him in Washington, and remained with his father for some time more. On the 25th, Grant wrote Julia, "Jess runs about the house loose and seeing the guests at meals thinks each time it is a new meal and that he must necessarily eat. In this way he eats five or six times each day and dips largely into deserts. If not looked after he will make himself sick," and asked if Fred had made it home yet.

19 Ibid., vol. 11, 97.

20 Ibid., 226. According to his father, Fred was suffering from rheumatism, fistula, and other "ailings."

which, according to the general's aide Horace Porter, Grant was seen wrestling with his children.[21]

Julia, Fred, and Jesse went to City Point for Christmas, 1864, and Fred visited his Uncle Fred Dent, and other generals and officers of his acquaintance, by some of whom he was affectionately called "The Veteran."[22] He also decided to go duck hunting, an adventure described by Horace Porter:

As sporting-guns are not found among army supplies, Fred had to content himself with an infantry rifled musket. The general's colored servant, Bill [Barnes], accompanied the boy. Bill was not much of a shot himself. He usually shot as many a man votes, with his eyes shut. But he was a good hand to take the place of the armor-bearer of the ancients, and carry the weapons. Taking a boat, they paddled down the [James] river in search of game. They had not gone far when they were brought to by the naval pickets who had been posted on the river-bank by the commander of one of the vessels. A picket-boat was sent after them, and they were promptly arrested as rebel spies, and taken aboard a gunboat. The declaration by the white prisoner, who, it was supposed, was plotting death and destruction to the Union, that he was the son of the general-in-chief, was at first deemed too absurd to be entertained by sailors, and fit only to be told to the marines; but after a time Fred succeeded in convincing the officers as to his identity, and was allowed to return to headquarters. When he arrived he wore a rueful expression of countenance at the thought of the ingratitude of republics to their "veterans." His father was greatly amused by the account of his adventure, teased him good-naturedly, and told him how fortunate it was that he had not been hanged at the yard-arm as an enemy of the republic, and his body consigned to the waters of the Potomac.[23]

Thus ended Fred's adventures during the Civil War.

---

21 Horace Porter, *Campaigning with Grant* (New York, 1897), 283–284.

22 Grant, *Papers*, vol. 13, 27, 54, 135, 152–153, 163, 167–168, 203; Porter, *Campaigning with Grant*, 363.

23 Porter, *Campaigning with Grant*, 365–366.

## FRED GRANT'S WARTIME MOVEMENTS[24]

### 1861

Early in the year: Fred and the family were home in Galena, Illinois.

June 22–24: Fred accompanied Grant from Galena to Camp Yates, near Springfield, Illinois.

July 3: Fred and Grant moved with the regiment west from Camp Yates.

July 4: Fred and Grant passed through Jacksonville, Illinois.

July 5: Fred and Grant camped at Allinson's Grove.

By July 9: Fred and Grant were at Camp Gardner on the west side of the Illinois River.

July 11: Fred and Grant arrived at Quincy on the Mississippi River.

July 12: Fred boarded a steamer at Quincy to Dubuque and, having missed his connecting train, walked 18 miles to Galena.

July–December: Fred was with his mother in Galena, with occasional visits to Grant at his headquarters at Cairo, including Christmas.

### 1862

About Feb. 1: Julia & the children left Cairo.

Feb. 10: Fred arrived at Grant's HQ at Fort Henry, leaving before February 14.

Feb. 22: Julia and the children arrived in Covington, Kentucky, where Grant's parents lived.

March–July: Julia and the children were in Louisville, Kentucky, with her aunt Emily Page, then returned to Covington, went to meet Grant at Corinth, and later traveled with him to Memphis.

July 13: Grant and the family went to Columbus, Kentucky

July 18: Julia and the children were in Jackson, Tennessee, and then joined Grant at Corinth.

August 16: Julia and the children left Corinth for St. Louis.

September: Julia left the older children with their paternal grandparents in Covington, where Fred attended school until early 1863.

---

24 Compiled chiefly from U. S. Grant's *Papers*, Mrs. Grant's *Personal Memoirs*, and Fred Grant's various writings.

## 1863

Early March: Fred left Covington with his mother and siblings for Nashville, then on to Memphis.

Late March: Fred took a steamer from Memphis, in company with Col. William S. Hillyer.

March 29: Fred arrived at Grant's headquarters, on a steamboat at Young's Point, Louisiana.

March 30: Fred accompanied Grant on an inspection of the canal.

April 1: Fred remained aboard the USS *Ivy* as Grant and other officers reconnoitered up the Yazoo River.

April 3: Grant's headquarters (and inferentially Fred) moved upstream to Milliken's Bend.

April 16: Fred accompanied Grant and the rest of the family on the *Henry Van Phul* to witness Porter's ironclads run past the Vicksburg batteries.

April 17: The *Henry Van Phul* returned to Milliken's Bend.

April 18: Fred accompanied Grant on horseback to visit McClernand's headquarters, reaching Richmond, Louisiana.

April 19: Fred and Grant arrived at McClernand's headquarters at New Carthage, LA.

April 20: Fred and Grant returned to Milliken's Bend.

April 24: Grant reconnoitered Grand Gulf; Fred's presence is uncertain.

Late April: Grant's headquarters, with Fred, moved via Richmond to Hard Times.

April 27: Grant's birthday, which Fred never mentions.

April 29: Fred accompanied Grant aboard a tug to observe a naval bombardment of Grand Gulf, then accompanies him to visit the USS *Benton*, where the general conferred with Admiral Porter.

April 30: Fred accompanied Grant aboard the captured *General Price* and witnessed troops being ferried across the river to Bruinsburg, remaining aboard when his father followed the troops.

May 1: Unaccompanied, Fred went ashore, witnessed the battle of Port Gibson, met Charles Dana at the Prentiss Plantation, each acquiring a horse, and was reunited with Grant that night.

May 2: Fred followed Grant on horseback to Port Gibson, then accompanied General Logan to see the remnants of the Confederates retreat, then rode to the North Fork, where his horse tripped, injuring Fred's leg.

May 3: Fred accompanied Grant across the North Fork Creek to Grand Gulf, where they went aboard the *Benton*.

May 4: Fred was left with Colonel Lagow while Grant went on ahead to the front.

May 5: Fred accompanied Colonel Lagow to Rocky Springs, where Grant was.

May 6: Fred followed the troops until he met his father.

May 7–12: Fred accompanied Grant on visits to corps commanders Sherman, McClernand, and McPherson.

May 12: Battle of Raymond. Fred accompanied "Pony" across Fourteen Mile Creek.

May 13: Fred rode into Raymond, Mississippi.

May 14: Fred accompanied Grant to Jackson, the capital of Mississippi, witnessed the battle, took part in the occupation of the city, helped capture the state capital, picked up some souvenirs, and then witnessed the burning of military installations and stores.

May 15: Fred accompanied Grant to Clinton, Mississippi.

May 16: Fred continued with Grant to Champion's farm, where a fierce battle was fought.

May 17: Fred accompanied Grant to the Big Black River, where he was nicked in the left thigh by a bullet.

May 18: Fred accompanied Grant across the Big Black River to Walnut Hills, on the outer works of Vicksburg, then joined Logan's division in camp.

May 19: With Vicksburg surrounded, Grant (possibly with Fred) spent the day inspecting the troops and the siege lines and observed the first attempt to storm the city.

May 22: Fred accompanied Grant to Logan's headquarters in front of Fort Hill on the Jackson Road, where he witnessed an artillery battle and later the unsuccessful second attempt to storm the city.

May 23–July 3: During this period of the siege of Vicksburg Fred apparently remained mostly in camp, recovering from his leg wound and various ailments.

May 30: Fred's birthday, which he doesn't mention.

June 25: Fred witnessed the explosion of the first Union mine.

Late June: Fred accompanied Grant on a tour of the Union lines from Haines's Bluff to the Big Black.

July 3: Fred accompanied Grant to Fort Hill, and then went with Gen. A. J. Smith and Colonel Lagow to receive Confederate officers under a flag of truce.

July 4: Fred accompanied Grant to the Jackson Road, for the formal surrender of Vicksburg, watched the Confederates stacking arms, then toured the city.

July 5: Grant moved into the Lum house in Vicksburg.

July 8: Fred left Vicksburg for St. Louis, arriving a few days later.

July–December: Fred attended school in St. Louis. Meanwhile his mother and young brother Jess stayed with Grant at Vicksburg until October. They then went to Cincinnati, and in November to her uncle's house in Louisville, Kentucky, through the end of the year, with a side trip to see Grant in Nashville in the third week of December.

Late December: Fred became gravely ill in St. Louis.

## 1864

January: Julia went to St. Louis, where Fred was suffering from camp dysentery and typhoid.

January 27: Receiving permission to leave the front, Grant arrived at St. Louis to find that Fred "has passed the crisis of his disease, and is considered out of danger . . . but is so much reduced that it will take months to restore him to his strength." Surprisingly, Fred recovered soon after being administered "nox vomica."[25]

Late February: Julia and Fred went to Nashville to see Grant, who wrote "Fred is . . . quite recovered."

Early March: Fred joined Grant at Chattanooga.

25 "Nux vomica" is a homeopathic remedy made from the seeds of the strychnine tree, which is native to south and southeast Asia. "In low doses, nux vomica increases glandular secretion in the gastrointestinal tract, and it has been used as a homeopathic remedy to stimulate digestion and treat a variety of gastrointestinal conditions," but is potentially dangerous. "Strychnos nux-vomica L.," United States Department of Agriculture, Natural Resources Conservation Service, https://plants. sc.egov.usda.gov/home/plantProfile?symbol=STNU4, accessed March 28, 2022; "Nux vomica," APA Dictionary of Psychology, https://dictionary.apa.org/nux-vomica.

March 5: Fred left Chattanooga with Grant.

March 8: Fred and Grant arrived in Washington, D.C., registered at the Willard Hotel.

March 9: Fred accompanied Grant to the White House, where his father received his commission as lieutenant general and conferred with military and political leaders.

Late March: His mother and Jess having arrived in Washington, Fred was sent back to school in St. Louis.

Late June: Fred went to City Point, Virginia to be with Grant for a few days, leaving due to health, the general writing that "between rheumatism, phistulo and other ailings I do not think he will ever do much active duty."

August 27: Grant traveled from City Point to Fort Monroe, where Julia and the children were living.

August 28: Grant returned to City Point with Julia and the children.

August 31: Grant accompanied Julia and the children from City Point to Fort Monroe.

By Sept. 5: Julia and the children were in Philadelphia, at the Continental Hotel, seeking to find a house.

Sept.–Dec: Julia and the children settled in a house in Burlington, NJ, where Fred and his siblings attended school, and they were occasionally visited by Grant.

December 24: Fred traveled to Washington on his way to visit Grant.

December 25: Fred arrived at City Point, Virginia, Grant's headquarters.

December 27: Fred went with his uncle Fred Dent to see General Ord.

## 1865

January 1–May: Fred returned from City Point to Burlington, where he attended school until after Appomattox, with occasional visits with his father.

## FRED GRANT AFTER THE CIVIL WAR

After the war Fred attended West Point, where he seems to have been peripherally involved in the hazing of cadet James Webster Smith, the first African American admitted to the academy. Graduating in 1871, Fred was commissioned a second lieutenant in the 4th Cavalry. He immediately went on leave to work as an engineer for a railroad and was then assigned as an aide-de-camp to Gen. William T. Sherman on his tour of the Mediterranean and Europe.[26] Returning in 1872, Fred rejoined his regiment in West Texas, but the following year he was promoted to lieutenant colonel and an aide-de-camp to Lt. Gen. Philip Sheridan. He later served on the frontier, accompanied his father on the former president's world tour (1877–1878), took part in the Bannock War in the Pacific northwest (1878) and in Victorio's War against the Apache (1879–1880). He resigned from the army in 1881 to enter business and then helped his father with his memoirs. Fred later engaged in business and dabbled in politics in New York State. He served as U.S. Minister to Austria-Hungary (1889–1893) and then became a member of the New York City Police Commission (1894–1898).

Fred returned to active duty for the Spanish-American War, briefly as colonel of the 14th New York National Guard Infantry (the "14th Brooklyn"), and then as a brigadier general of volunteers.[27] After that war's conclusion he was for a time military commander of Puerto Rico and then commanded a brigade which included the African American 25th Infantry, during the Filipino-American War (1899–1902).[28] Promoted to brigadier general in the regular army, he held various assignments, rising to major general in 1906 and in 1911 became the second highest ranking officer in the army, commanding the Division of the East, encompassing most of the United States east of the Mississippi. He died in 1912 of cancer at Fort Jay, on Governor's Island in New York Harbor.

In 1874, Fred had married Ida Marie Honoré (1854–1930), daughter of a Chicago real estate baron, and the couple had two children. Their eldest, daughter Julia Dent Grant (1876–1975), married Russian Prince Mikhail Cantacuzène

---

26 Sherman, *Memoirs*, II:451–452.

27 Fred commanded the 1st Division of the Third Army Corps. "Passing in Review at Chickamauga, the New York Regiments Showed Off to Advantage," *New York Times*, June 4, 1898, 3; "Gen. Fred Grant's Battle; The Event of the Week at Chickamauga Was the Sham Engagement Under His Direction," *New York Times*, June 26, 1898, 9.

28 A motion picture clip of Grant leading the 25th Infantry exists, see "Gen. Frederick D. Grant and Gen. A. S. Burt [commander of the 25th Infantry Regiment] returning from Mt. Ariat [*sic*], at the head of the famous 25th Infantry, colored," is, available for download from the Library of Congress at https://www.loc.gov/item/98500744/.

Brig. Gen. Frederick D. Grant and Mrs. Ida Marie Honoré Grant, c. 1905.
*Library of Congress*

(1875–1955), a general and diplomat. She wrote several books about Russia during the waning years of the Tsarist regime. The second child, Ulysses S. Grant III (1881–1968), graduated from West Point in 1906, along with Douglas MacArthur. U. S. G. III married Edith Root (1878–1962), daughter of Secretary of State Elihu Root, who was later a senator from New York. An engineer, U. S. G. III served in Cuba, on the Mexican border, and in World War I was an aide to the Allied Supreme War Council. During the Coolidge administration he oversaw conversion of the White House attic into a fourth floor. In World War II he served as deputy director of Civil Defense, under national director Fiorello La Guardia. He retired from the Army as a major general in 1946. U. S. G. III belonged to the District of Columbia Civil War Roundtable, headed the Military Order of the Loyal Legion of the United States (an organization of Union officers and their the descendants), chaired the national Civil War Centennial Commission until August 1962, and spoke at his grandfather's tomb in New York at the opening of the Centennial events on January 8, 1961, and at Appomattox Court House on April 9, 1965.

Maj. Gen. Frederick D. Grant with aviator James J. ("Jimmie") Ward in New York prior
to the Hearst Transcontinental Flight, which started from Governor's Island.

*National Archives*

# APPENDIX I

# PERSONS MENTIONED
# IN THE TEXT

The principal references for most of the soldiers Fred Grant mentions in his memoir are Ezra Warner's *Generals in Gray* and *Generals in Blue*, the 1903 edition of Francis B. Heitman's *Historical Register and Dictionary of the United States Army, 1789–1903* (generally known as "Heitman's Register"), Rodger D. Hunt's and Jack R. Brown's *Brevet Brigadier Generals in Blue*, Rodger D. Hunt's series *Colonels in Blue*, and Bruce S. Allardice's *Confederate Colonels*. For fuller citations to these and other personnel references, see the Bibliography.

Banks, Nathaniel P. (1816–1894). From Massachusetts, upon finishing public school Banks worked in a textile mill—"Bobbin Boy Banks"—and as a mechanic's apprentice, read voraciously, and became an able debater and orator. Entering politics as a Democrat, he served in the state legislature and Congress, becoming speaker of the house, and then governor of his state. Staunchly Unionist, Lincoln made him a major general of volunteers, the second such appointment in the war, and the first to a political figure. Banks had some skill as a general (almost defeating Stonewall Jackson at Cedar Mountain in August 1862), but as one biographer wrote, Banks "was cursed with too much rank too soon and never had the chance to go back and acquire the skills that his hasty promotion forced him to lead without."[1]

Barnes, George William (c. 1843–1908). Barnes was Grant's African-American servant, nicknamed "Bill." According to Horace Porter, who called him "a notable

---

1  James G. Hollandsworth Jr, *Pretense of Glory: The Life of General Nathaniel P. Banks* (Baton Rouge, 1999), 52.

character," Bill had escaped slavery in Missouri early in the war. Making his way to Cairo, Illinois, he attached himself to various officers as a personal attendant. When Bill's current charge, Col. George B. Boomer, was killed during the attempt to storm Vicksburg on May 22, 1863, he attached himself to Grant. Although Grant at times seems to have despaired of Bill's drinking, he proved so valuable that he continued to work for Grant through the end of the war and during his presidency. After trying his hand at business and preaching, through the influence of the Grant family he became a government messenger in Washington.[2]

Bell, Charles S. (1843–1879). A native of New York, in 1861 Bell joined the 19th Illinois Infantry but was discharged for health later that year. In September 1862 he became a scout for Maj. Gen. Stephen Hurlbut, commanding Union forces in western Tennessee and northern Mississippi. By war's end Bell is believed to have "logged at least thirty-seven missions behind enemy lines and traveled hundreds of miles in Missouri, Mississippi, Arkansas, Louisiana, Virginia, and Canada." In early 1863, he became a spy. Passing as "Lieutenant C. S. Pierson," Bell became an aide-de-camp to Brig. Gen. James R. Chalmers (1831–1898), the Confederate commander of northern Mississippi. In this guise Bell seems to have been one of three officers entrusted with Joe Johnston's directive to Pemberton to unite their armies. Bell informed Grant of this, who then ordered McPherson to move his troops to prevent the juncture, which precipitated the battle of the Big Black River Bridge on May 17th.[3]

Blair, Francis Preston, Jr. (1821–1875). Blair, the well-educated scion of a powerful political family, practiced law in Kentucky, went to Colorado, served in the Mexican War, became attorney general of the New Mexico territory, and then entered politics in Missouri as a Free Soiler and abolitionist, rising to national notice. Early in the Civil War he played an important role in keeping Missouri loyal to the Union and served on the Congressional Military Affairs Committee. In 1862 he raised seven regiments, became a brigadier general, and led a brigade in Missouri and on the Yazoo Expedition. Promoted to major general, he led a division during the Vicksburg campaign, at Chattanooga and in the early phases of the Atlanta campaign. He then commanded the Seventeenth Corps, leading it through the fall of Atlanta, on the March to the Sea, and in the Carolinas. Both Grant and Sherman considered Blair an excellent soldier. After the war he

2  Porter, *Campaigning with Grant*, 130*ff*.; Chernow, *Grant*, 642, 863; J. Fraise Richard, "Grant's Life Saved; Colored Servant in Need," *The Washington Bee*, May 27, 1911, 1; "George W. Barnes," *The Washington Bee*, June 27, 1908, 4.

3  William B. Feis, "Charles S. Bell: Union Scout," *North & South* 4 , no. 5 (June 2001): 26–37; Grant, *Personal Memoirs*, I:508.

Pictured here in a prewar militia uniform, Confederate Maj. Gen. John S. Bowen brought Pemberton's request for surrender negotiations to Grant.
*Library of Congress*

abandoned his earlier political views, became a Democrat and a senator, and opposed Reconstruction and equal rights for African Americans.

Bowen, John Stevens (1830–1863). A native of Georgia, Bowen graduated from West Point in 1853. Commissioned in the Mounted Rifles (now the 3rd Cavalry), he resigned in 1856 and became an architect in St. Louis, where he became acquainted with Grant. A lieutenant colonel in the state militia, in 1861 he supported the Confederacy, becoming colonel of the 1st Missouri, and then commanded a brigade. Promoted to brigadier, he ably led a brigade at Shiloh, where he was seriously wounded, then at Corinth, and then under Pemberton in Mississippi. He fortified Grand Gulf and performed so well at Port Gibson that he was nominated for promotion to major general (though not confirmed, he was thenceforth referred to as such). He led a division at Champion Hill, the Big Black River, and in the defenses of Vicksburg. Ill with dysentery at the time of the surrender, he died shortly afterwards. Grant considered him an able commander.[4]

Bowers, Theodore S. (1832–1866). A newspaperman, Bowers served as a first lieutenant in the 48th Illinois; then captain and aide-de-camp to Grant; major and then judge advocate of the Army of Tennessee; and lieutenant colonel and assistant adjutant general to Grant. Breveted to brigadier general in 1865, he then served as a colonel in the regular army until killed in a railroad accident.[5]

Breese, Kidder Randolph (1831–1881). A midshipman in the Mexican War, Breese was commissioned in 1852, went to Japan with Commodore Perry

4  Grant, *Papers*, vol. 8, 147.

5  "The Late Colonel Bowers," *Harper's Weekly*, March 24, 1866.

Lt. Cdr. Kidder R. Breese, U.S.N.
*U.S. Navy History and Heritage Command*

(1852–1855), and served on expeditions to Paraguay (1858) and Panama (1859). A lieutenant at the start of the war, he commanded gunboats on the Mississippi, the mortar fleet during the bombardment of Forts St. Philip and Jackson below New Orleans (April 1862) and was Porter's "fleet captain" (chief-of-staff) for the rest of the war, though in January of 1865 he commanded the navy-marine brigade during the storming of Fort Fisher, off Wilmington, North Carolina.

Buchanan, Robert Christie (1811–1878). A native Marylander and nephew-in-law to President John Quincy Adams, Buchanan graduated from West Point in 1830 and was commissioned in the 4th Infantry, which U. S. Grant would join in 1843. He served in the Black Hawk War, the Seminole Wars, "Indian Removal," and in the war with Mexico, winning brevets to major and lieutenant colonel. In 1853, while commanding elements of the 4th Infantry on the northern California coast, he accused Grant of excessive drinking. Recalled east when the Civil War began, he was promoted to lieutenant colonel and commanded a brigade of regulars ably in the Peninsular campaign, Second Bull Run, Antietam, and Fredericksburg. But he ran afoul of Army politics and was denied promotion to brigadier general, ending the war in various administrative posts. He died on active duty, as a colonel with a brevet to brigadier general.

Burbridge, Stephen G. (1831–1894). A Kentucky attorney, planter, and slave owner, Burbridge began the war as colonel of the Unionist 26th Kentucky. A controversial officer, he rose to brigadier general, and during the Vicksburg campaign commanded a brigade in the Thirteenth Army Corps. He was the first senior Union officer to receive Pemberton's delegates requesting surrender negotiations. He later earned a reputation for brutality while commanding the military district of Kentucky and resigned from the army shortly after the war.

Pictured here in civilian dress, probably postwar, Maj. Gen. Stephen G. Burbridge was the first senior Union officer to receive Pemberton's truce negotiators.

*Library of Congress*

Cadle, Cornelius (1836–1913). Cadle, a 1st Lieutenant in the 11th Iowa, was attached to Brigadier General Crocker's staff and later rose to lieutenant colonel. Cadle mustered out of the service on July 6th, two days after the fall of Vicksburg.[6]

Crocker, Marcellus M. (1830–1865). A native of Indiana, Crocker briefly attended West Point but left to become a lawyer in Iowa. In 1861 he was a captain in the 2nd Iowa Infantry, by year's end a colonel of the 13th Iowa. At Shiloh he assumed command of a brigade under fire, led it at Second Corinth, was promoted to brigadier general, and took part in Grant's operations against Vicksburg, rising to division command. Suffering from consumption, after the fall of Vicksburg he was sent to New Mexico in hope of recovering his health, but never returned to field service. He died in Washington in August of 1865. Grant considered him one of the best division commanders in the army.[7]

Dana, Charles A. (1819–1897). A veteran reporter and later managing editor of the *New York Tribune*, in late 1862 Dana was appointed a special agent by Secretary of War Stanton to report on military operations in the Western theater. He arrived at Grant's headquarters on April 6th. In late 1863 he became assistant secretary of war. After the war he was part owner and editor of the *New York Sun*. A prolific author of both fiction and non-fiction, his posthumously published *Recollections of the Civil War: With Leaders at Washington and in the Field in the Sixties* (New York, 1898), which offers many valuable insights and anecdotes.

6  See *O.R.*,XXIV, 1, 723–724; Cadwallader, *Three Years with Grant*, 75; Edwin C. Bearss and Warren Grabau, *The Battle of Jackson, May 14, 1863. The Siege of Jackson, July 10–17, 1863. Three Other Post-Vicksburg Actions* (Baltimore, 1981), 26.

7  Grant, *Personal Memoirs*, I:497–498.

Dent, Frederick T. (1820–1892). Scion of a slave-holding Missouri family, Dent was U. S. Grant's classmate at West Point and later his brother-in-law. Commissioned in the cavalry, he won two brevets in Mexico and spent most of his career on the frontier. Loyal to the Union, he saw little service in the Civil War until early 1864, when he was promoted to lieutenant colonel and aide-de-camp to Grant, ending the war as a brigadier general of volunteers. After the war he was promoted to that rank in the regular army. He served as Grant's military secretary during the latter's presidency. Fred Grant was named after him.

Durant, D. Blakely (1826–1894). A free-born African American, Durant became a cook for the officers' mess of the 71st Ohio in February 1862. He served at Fort Donelson and Shiloh, where he was credited with rescuing the colors from the regiment's hastily abandoned camp. After Shiloh he was "chief caterer" to McPherson's staff and cooked for Grant often while he was at Milliken's Bend. In camp, Durant often sang "Old Shady," a song celebrating escape from slavery (which he disclaimed having written), which became quite popular. It's sometimes said his nickname was derived from the song, or vice versa. He left the army in December of 1863, returned to Ohio, and began catering on steamboats. Postwar he eventually settled in Grand Forks, North Dakota. Durant was given a splendid funeral, escorted by the local GAR and militia.[8]

Dwight, William (1831–1888). From a distinguished Massachusetts family, Dwight attended a military prep school, then West Point in 1849, but was discharged for "deficiency in studies" in early 1853 just months before graduation. Entering business in Massachusetts and later Pennsylvania, on the outbreak of the war he was commissioned lieutenant colonel in the 70th New York, commanded by the notorious Daniel Sickles. Wounded and left for dead at Williamsburg, he was captured (May 5, 1862). After being exchanged he was made a brigadier general of volunteers, commanded a brigade in Nathaniel Banks's army at Port Hudson, became Banks's chief-of-staff, then led a division badly in the Shenandoah Valley. Reputedly a looter and shirker, he was not awarded a brevet at war's end.

Grierson, Benjamin H. (1826–1911). A native of Pennsylvania, as a child Grierson was nearly killed by a horse, and as a result was not fond of them. As a young man he studied music and became a music teacher and band leader in Illinois. Early in the war a volunteer aide-de-camp to Maj. Gen. Benjamin M. Prentiss, in October 1861 he joined the 6th Illinois Cavalry as a major, became colonel of the regiment the following spring, and then commanded a cavalry brigade in the Army of the Tennessee. After leading his famous raid (see p. 9, note 10), he was promoted to brigadier general of volunteers and supported the siege of

---

8  For the song, see Appendix IV.

Port Hudson. He then commanded a cavalry division in anti-partisan operations, conducted a second major raid across Mississippi, and took part in the capture of Mobile. After the war he commanded the 10th Cavalry ("The Buffalo Soldiers") for more than two decades. A strong supporter of the professionalism of African American troops, he was friendly with Native Americans. Grierson retired in 1890 as a brigadier general in the regular army, with a brevet for major general. Despite his aversion to horses, he was among the best horse soldiers in the war.

Griffith, Joseph Evan (1843–1877). Born in Wales, Griffith's family arrived in the U.S. in 1849 and moved to Iowa in 1855, where he became a teacher and grocer. He joined the 22nd Iowa in mid-1862, rising quickly to sergeant. Although commissioned a lieutenant, he resigned to enter West Point in October 1863, graduating in 1867, fifth in his class. Commissioned a 2nd lieutenant of engineers, he engaged in improvements to navigation on the Great Lakes and rivers. Honorably discharged at his request in 1870, he worked in engineering and mining until his death in Iowa.

Hains, Peter Conover (1840–1921). Hains graduated West Point in June 1861. Commissioned in the artillery, he transferred to the Topographical Engineers and then the Engineers by early 1863. Chief engineer of McClernand's corps during the Vicksburg campaign, he was very active during the siege of the city, earning one of his three brevets for the Civil War. He later wrote several papers about the campaign. He later rose to brigadier general of volunteers during the Spanish-American War in 1898, then also in the Regular Army. Retiring in 1904, he was promoted to major general on the retired list in 1916. Recalled to active duty the following year for World War I, he retired once more in 1918, one of several Civil War veterans who served in the Great War. His son, army captain Peter Conover Hains II, was involved in a notorious murder, and his grandson, Peter Conover Hains III, served as an armor/cavalry officer in World War II and later rose to major general.

Halleck, Henry Wager (1815–1872). From upstate New York, Halleck ranked 3rd in the West Point class of 1839. Commissioned in the engineers, he worked on the defenses of New York City, read voraciously in military literature, and began to write. Sent to study European military trends in 1844–1845, upon returning he wrote *Elements of Military Art and Science* and translated Antoine-Henri Jomini's biography of Napoleon into English. He served in California during the war with Mexico, earning a brevet. Leaving the Army as a captain in 1854, Halleck entered politics and business in California, becoming quite wealthy. Appointed a major general in August 1861, he proved a very able administrator, but a poor field commander. Made general-in-chief in mid-1862, he often meddled in Grant's operations, apparently prompted by rumors of the latter's drinking. When

1st Lt. Peter C. Hains, Chief Engineer
of the Thirteenth Army Corps
*Library of Congress*

Grant became general-in-chief in early 1864, Halleck became chief-of-staff of the army, in which post he proved quite able. His nicknames "Old Brains" and "Old Wooden Head" perfectly reflect his personality.

Hewit, Henry Stuart (1825–1873). A native of Connecticut, Hewit was appointed an assistant surgeon (medical lieutenant) in 1849. Hewit resigned in 1851 to practice medicine in California, and from 1855 in New York. He became a surgeon (medical captain) in the U.S. Volunteers on August 3, 1861, and was attached to Grant's staff in 1862. His work with the wounded at Jackson left him exhausted and ill, and he went north on sick leave. Captured en route, he was held in Libby Prison for a time. Sent north without parole to attend a group of wounded men being exchanged, he went on medical leave. Upon recovery, he returned to Grant's headquarters, creating some difficulties, as his orders were to report to Annapolis, Maryland. The matter required attention from Grant in October 1863. Hewit ran a hospital at Frederick, Maryland, until mustering out in October 1865, with brevets for lieutenant colonel and colonel. Returning to medicine in New York, he was active in medical and civic organizations until his death. Shortly after his death, then-President Grant recommended his son for admission to the Naval Academy.[9]

Hillyer, William Silliman, Sr. (1831–1874). Kentucky-born but raised in Indiana, Hillyer was practicing law in St. Louis when he met U. S. Grant in the late 1850s. Briefly serving in Unionist Missouri forces very early in the war, in mid-1861 he joined Grant's staff as a captain, serving at Belmont, Donelson, Shiloh (where he briefly commanded a brigade), and during the protracted operations against Vicksburg, rising to colonel. He resigned shortly before the fall of Vicksburg, due to declining health. Later breveted a brigadier general, after the war he held various government appointments. Grant was at his bedside when he died, the last survivor of Grant's wartime staff. Hillyer had accompanied Fred from

9 Grant, *Papers*, vol. 9, 261–252; vol. 23, 17–18; "Obituary. Henry Stewart Hewit, M.D.," *The Medical Record*, Sept. 1, 1873, 462.

Brig. Gen. Alvin Peterson Hovey commanded a division in the Thirteenth Army Corps.
*Library of Congress*

Memphis to Young's Point, bringing along his 10-year-old son, William S. Hillyer Jr. (see page 8, note 4) who had already been with him in the field several times.

Hillyer, William Silliman, Jr. (1853–1885). The son of Col. Hillyer, Hillyer Jr. spent considerable time with the army, and had been appointed by Grant as "Pony Aid de Camp" on November 1, 1861. In a letter dated November 27, 1864, responding to an invitation from young Hillyer to visit his school, Grant addressed him as "My little friend." As an adult he worked for the Customs Service in New York.[10]

Hovey, Alvin Peterson (1821–1891). An Indiana native orphaned at 15, Hovey endured extreme poverty, laid bricks, studied law, and became a successful attorney. Entering politics as a reform Democrat, he helped write a new state constitution, served briefly on the state supreme court, was U.S. attorney for Indiana, and became a Republican in the late 1850s. When the war began, he became a colonel in the state militia, then led the 24th Indiana Infantry at Shiloh, winning a promotion to brigadier general of volunteers. He commanded brigades and then a division in the Thirteenth Army Corps, distinguishing himself at Champion Hill, and later on campaign in eastern Tennessee and Kentucky. He ended the war as commander of the Military District of Indiana, with a brevet to major general. After the war he served as U.S. minister to Peru, a member of Congress, and governor of Indiana.

Howe, Orion Perseus (1848–1931). An Ohio native, Howe's family moved to Illinois by 1855. He enlisted in the 55th Illinois Infantry as a drummer on September 1, 1862, with his father William Harrison Howe (1820–1901) as principal musician and brother Lyston Druett (1850–1937), also a drummer. As noted in Fred's account, Hovey was wounded on May 19, 1863, during the

10 Grant, *Papers*, vol. 3, 120; Ibid., 32, 69.

Vicksburg campaign and was several months in recovery. Promoted to corporal on December 25, 1863, he was wounded again on May 28, 1864, at Dallas, near Atlanta, and was discharged on October 1, 1864. General Sherman recommended him for an appointment to West Point, but he entered the Naval Academy in 1865. Dropping out, he became a merchant seaman and was shipwrecked off the Irish coast in 1867. He later became a cowboy and served as an army scout in the Great Sioux War of 1876, before settling in Missouri. In 1896 he was awarded the Medal of Honor for his courageous actions at Vicksburg, among the youngest recipients of the decoration.[11]

Johnston, Joseph Eggleston (1807–1891). Johnston, a Virginian, graduated West Point in 1829. He served in the artillery, and later the Topographical Engineers, in the Second Seminole War (1837–1838), winning a brevet. A lieutenant colonel of volunteers in the Mexican War (1846–1848), he won two brevets. In 1855 he became lieutenant colonel of the new 1st Cavalry Regiment (now the 4th Cavalry), and in 1860 became quartermaster general of the army, ranking as a brigadier general. He became a full general in Confederate service. Naturally cautious, some contemporaries—and some modern historians—charge that Johnston's actions during the Vicksburg campaign were primarily intended to avoid blame for the eventual loss of the city. Grant, however, regarded him highly. Johnston maintained a contentious relationship with many of his subordinates and with Jefferson Davis.[12]

Lagow, Clark Breading (1828–1867). An Illinois native, Lagow mustered in for three years as a first lieutenant in the 21st Illinois Infantry, on June 3, 1861. Grant, then regimental commander, soon appointed him an aide-de-camp. Lagow thereafter was on Grant's staff in all his operations through the Chattanooga campaign, as captain (by February 1862) and colonel (from May 3, 1862). He was in operational command of the transports that ran the Vicksburg batteries on April 22, 1863. Grant initially found him an able officer, and called him "a true, honest man, willing to do all in his power for the service," but seems to have become dissatisfied with him later. Lagow resigned from the service in December 1863 rather than be dismissed. Whatever the issue was, Grant approved Lagow's promotion to brevet brigadier general of volunteers at the end of the war.[13]

Lauman, Jacob Gartner (1813–1867). A successful businessman in Iowa, Lauman began raising troops in mid-1861. Named colonel of the 7th Iowa in

---

11 *The Story of the Fifty-fifth Regiment Illinois Volunteer Infantry in the Civil War, 1861–1865* (Clinton, MA, 1887), 43, 54, 237, 239ff; The Census of 1860 spells the young man's name as "Orien."

12 Bearss and Grabau, *Jackson*, 130.

13 *O.R.*, LII, 1, 314; *O.R.*, XXXI, 2, 54; *O.R.*, XXIV, 1, 31, 566–567; Official Army Register for 1863 (Washington, D.C., 1863), 62.

Union Maj. Gen. Jacob Gartner Lauman,
"a very good man but a very poor general."
*Library of Congress*

July, he led it at Belmont (November 7, 1861), where he was severely wounded. He commanded a brigade at Fort Donelson, then, after a promotion to brigadier general of volunteers, at Shiloh, Hatchie's Bridge, and against Earl Van Dorn in west Tennessee. During the Vicksburg campaign Lauman led a division in the Sixteenth Army Corps, and then in the Thirteenth Army Corps. Described by Dana as "a very good man but a very poor general," during the capture of Jackson, Mississippi, in July 1863, he was relieved by Ord and Sherman for failing to properly carry out orders and held no further command. Brevetted major general of volunteers at the end of the war, he long suffered from the effects of his Belmont wound. Lauman resumed business and tried unsuccessfully to clear his record. His name is sometimes found as Laumann and Lawman.

Leggett, Mortimer Dormer (1821–1896). Raised in Ohio, Leggett practiced law and taught in public schools there, playing a role in the introduction of the graded school concept. On the eve of the war he was superintendent of schools in Zanesville. Early in the war he served as a volunteer aide-de-camp to George McClellan in western Virginia, then became lieutenant colonel of the 78th Ohio Infantry. Soon rising to colonel, he commanded the regiment at Fort Donelson, Shiloh, and Corinth, and was promoted to brigadier general of volunteers in November 1862. During the Vicksburg campaign he commanded a brigade in McPherson's corps, but on June 25th the detonation of a mine on his front caused him permanent injury. Returning to duty despite partial disability, he commanded a division in the Atlanta campaign, the March to the Sea, and the Carolinas campaign, ending the war as a major general of volunteers. After the war he returned to the law, served for a time as U.S. Commissioner of Patents, and founded a company that later merged into General Electric.

Shown here as a major general, Mortimer Dormer Leggett was seriously wounded commanding a Union brigade during the campaign.
*Library of Congress*

Logan, John Alexander (1826–1886). Logan, an Illinois native, served in the Mexican War, practiced law in his home state, became a Douglas Democrat, and entered Congress. He was a volunteer combatant at Bull Run, Belmont, and Fort Donelson, where he was wounded. Resigning from Congress in April 1862, he became colonel of the 31st Illinois and was promptly promoted to brigadier general. Logan led a brigade at Corinth, then a division in the Army of the Tennessee, rising to major general. Military governor of Vicksburg upon its capture, in late 1863 he commanded the Fifteenth Army Corps through the fall of Atlanta (and temporarily the Army of the Tennessee on McPherson's death) and later in the Carolinas. He then commanded the Army of the Tennessee from May through August of 1865, including the Grand Review in Washington. After the war a Radical Republican, in the House and then the Senate, he was engaged in bitter political battles. Later commander of the Grand Army of the Republic, he helped establish Decoration Day (Memorial Day) as a holiday in many states. Logan was considered an excellent commander by Grant and Sherman.

Maloney, Maurice (c. 1812–1872). Born in Ireland, Maloney joined the 4th Infantry Regiment as a private in 1836 and rose to sergeant major, fighting in the Seminole War. Commissioned second lieutenant in the regiment for the Mexican War in 1846 (two brevets), he rose to captain. In October 1861, he became colonel of the 13th Wisconsin, but in September 1862 returned to the regular army as a major in the 1st Infantry. He earned two brevets during the Civil War, one for Vicksburg, and retired as a lieutenant colonel in 1870.

McClernand, John Alexander (1812–1900). An Illinois attorney, member of Congress, and a Douglas Democrat, McClernand raised a volunteer brigade in 1861 and was commissioned a brigadier general of volunteers. He served with some ability under Grant at Donelson and Shiloh and commanded the Thirteenth

Army Corps during the Vicksburg campaign. McClernand frequently clashed with his colleagues, was insubordinate, lied, and was openly critical of Grant and other senior commanders to political leaders, including Lincoln. A series of blunders caused Grant to relieve him in mid-June 1863. Wary of offending McClernand's supporters in Illinois, Lincoln sidelined him with a command on the Gulf coast.

McPherson, James Birdseye (1828–1864). McPherson, an Ohioan, graduated from West Point in 1853, first in his class. Commissioned in the engineers, he worked on fortifications in the East and then at Alcatraz, rising to captain. At San Francisco when the war began, he postponed his wedding, applied for transfer to the East, and was shortly a lieutenant colonel and assistant aide-de-camp to Maj. Gen. Henry Halleck at St. Louis. Chief engineer to Grant in the Henry-Donelson, Shiloh, and Corinth campaigns, he rose to brigadier general of volunteers. Promoted to major general of volunteers in December 1862, he commanded the Seventeenth Army Corps during the Vicksburg, Chattanooga, and Meridian campaigns. During the Atlanta campaign he commanded the Army of the Tennessee until July 22, 1864, when he was killed during the battle of Atlanta while trying to escape capture by troops commanded by his former West Point roommate, John Bell Hood. Widely considered the best younger officer in the Army, he was greatly mourned, Grant reportedly shedding tears on hearing the news. His fiancé Emily Hoffman never married.

Montgomery, Louis M. (c. 1834–1916). A New York-born attorney, journalist, author, and lyricist, Montgomery mustered into Confederate service at New Orleans in May 1861 as color sergeant of the Washington Artillery of Louisiana and served in the Army of Northern Virginia. In February 1863 he was appointed captain and acting assistant adjutant general to Kirby Smith, in the Trans-Mississippi. Unable to reach Kirby Smith, he was attached to Pemberton as acting lieutenant colonel and aide-de-camp. Paroled after Vicksburg, in early 1864 he applied to President Davis for promotion and permission to raise a new unit but received no reply. After the war he lived abroad, working as a journalist, traveling widely, and apparently telling tall tales about himself. Returning to the U.S., he eventually became head of customs in New England and was a prominent anti-immigrant advocate.[14]

Oglesby, Richard James (1824–1899). A veteran of the war with Mexico, Oglesby prospered in California during the Gold Rush, then entered politics in his native Illinois. At the start of the Civil War, he became colonel of the 8th Illinois Infantry and served mostly under Grant. He rose to major general, serving

---

14 William M. Owen, *In Camp and Battle with the Washington Artillery of New Orleans* (Baton Rouge, 1999), 9, 19–20, 73, 109, 165.

Maj. Gen. E. O. C. Ord with his family.
*Library of Congress*

in northern Mississippi during the Vicksburg campaign. He left the army in early 1864 and became governor of Illinois.

Oliver, William Stockley (1836–1896). An Alabama-born St. Louis merchant and contractor, Oliver was commissioned a captain in the Unionist 7th Missouri in June 1861 and rose to colonel in April 1863. He and his men volunteered for duty in the second running of the batteries at Vicksburg. Oliver mustered out of the service in July 1864, resumed his business, served for a time as a sheriff in Arkansas, and died in Mexico.

Ord, Edward Otho Cresap (1818–1883). Born in Maryland, Ord graduated West Point in 1839. He served in the Seminole War in 1840, the Mexican War, and in the Pacific northwest (rising to captain), and participated in the suppression of John Brown's raid. In California at the outbreak of the war, he was promoted to brigadier general of volunteers and commanded brigades and then divisions in Virginia. He rose to major general, fighting at Corinth, Iuka, and the Hatchie River, where a severe wound put him out of action for months. He assumed command of the Thirteenth Army Corps when Grant relieved McClernand. Ord later served in the east, commanding the Army of the James in the final weeks of the war. Postwar he rose to major general in the regular army and retired in 1881.

Osterhaus, Peter Joseph (1823–1917). Born in Prussia, Osterhaus was an officer candidate in the Prussian army and was commissioned in a militia regiment. During the liberal uprisings of 1848–1849 he joined the revolutionaries as a colonel of volunteers at Mannheim. Fleeing Germany, he eventually settled in St. Louis. In 1861 he became a captain in the 2nd Missouri Volunteers, a "German" regiment, distinguishing himself at Wilson Creek in August. Shortly becoming colonel of the 12th Missouri (another "German" regiment), he again distinguished himself at Pea Ridge (March 7–8, 1862). Promoted to brigadier general of volunteers, he commanded a division during the Vicksburg, Chattanooga, and Atlanta campaigns, rose to major general of volunteers and command of the Fifteenth Army Corps during Sherman's "March to the Sea," ending the war as chief-of-staff to Maj. Gen. Edward Canby, in the Military Division of West Mississippi. After the war he was military governor of Mississippi for a time, then U.S. Consul in Lyon, France (1867–1877), including the period of the Franco-Prussian War. Returning to Prussia, he served for a time as U.S. Vice-Consul at Mannheim. He died in Prussia weeks before the U.S. entered World War I against Germany, in which his son and grandson served as U.S. naval officers.

Pemberton, John Clifford (1814–1881). A native Pennsylvanian, Pemberton graduated from West Point in 1837 and served in the artillery. During the Mexican War, he served alongside Grant, receiving two brevets, and shortly rose to captain. In 1861, having married into a prosperous slaveholding Virginia family, he joined the Confederacy. Despite the belief by some that he was a Unionist sympathizer, he rose quickly, and in October 1862 was a lieutenant general and commander of the Department of Mississippi and East Louisiana, with the mission of defending Vicksburg. Arguably Pemberton might have done better, but Johnston and Jefferson Davis kept issuing conflicting instructions. Idled for a time after the fall of Vicksburg, he reverted to lieutenant colonel of artillery and commanded the artillery defenses of Richmond until nearly the end of the war. After the war he lived for a time in Virginia and then returned to Pennsylvania. His family was staunchly Unionist, and he had two brothers in blue.

Porter, David Dixon (1813–1891). Porter was the son of naval hero and adventurer David Porter (1780–1843), who was guardian of the young David G. Farragut. The older Porter commanded the Mexican navy (1826–1829), in which young David became a midshipman at 12, serving under fire several times. Transferring to the U.S. Navy in 1829, Porter saw extensive service. A lieutenant by the eve of the Civil War, he soon became Lincoln's favorite naval officer. Aggressive, and possessing a terrific sense of humor, he supported innovation and became a noted reformer, rising to become the navy's second full admiral, after Farragut. A notorious looter, Porter authored the quite detailed and, some would say, tedious *The Naval History of the Civil War* and the very amusing *Incidents and Anecdotes of the Civil War*.

Ransom, Thomas Edwin Greenfield (1834–1864). Ransom was the son of Col. Truman B. Ransom (1802–1847), president of Norwich University, who was killed in action at Chapultepec, Mexico. After graduating from Norwich, Ransom became a civil engineer in Illinois. In April 1861 he raised Company E of the 11th Illinois Infantry, and by July was lieutenant colonel. He served in Missouri,

Brig. Gen. Thomas E. G. Ransom led a brigade in the Seventeenth Army Corps during the Vicksburg Campaign.
*Library of Congress*

commanded the regiment at Fort Donelson, rising to colonel, and at Shiloh, Corinth, and in operations in central Tennessee. Promoted to brigadier in November 1862, Ransom led a brigade in McPherson's Seventeenth Army Corps during the Vicksburg campaign, then rose to command the corps, and later the Sixteenth Arny Corps during the Atlanta campaign and operations in Georgia. Wounded four times in the war, he died of dysentery in October 1864, shortly after being brevetted major general.

Rawlins, John Aaron (1831–1869). Rawlins rose from poverty to become an attorney. A "War Democrat," he assisted Grant in organizing a volunteer company, which helped get Grant reinstated in the army. Commissioned, he served as an aide and later chief-of-staff to Grant through the war. In March of 1869, despite worsening tuberculosis, newly installed President Grant made Rawlins Secretary of War. Rawlins died five months later. A man "known for his command of profanity," he got along surprisingly well with the mild-tongued Grant.[15]

Sanborn, John Benjamin (1826–1904). A Minnesota lawyer and politician, Sanborn became state adjutant general in 1861 and then commanded the 4th Minnesota Volunteers. He led brigades at Corinth and Iuka, and with Grant during operations against Vicksburg, rising to division command. Appointed a brigadier after the fall of Vicksburg, he later held territorial commands in Missouri and ended the war with a brevet for major general. Postwar he served on the frontier until leaving the army in 1869, returning to business and politics in Minnesota.

Sherman, William Tecumseh (1820–1891). Foster son of prominent Whig politician Thomas Ewing Sr. (whose daughter he married), Sherman graduated West Point in 1840. He served in the Second Seminole War, on staff and administrative duty in Georgia and the Carolinas, and in California during the

---

15 White, *American Ulysses*, 139.

Mexican-American War, but did not see combat. After that war he left the army to become a banker in California, then in New York until the Panic of 1857. Later the first superintendent of what is now Louisiana State University, Sherman resigned soon after the state seceded. Managing a streetcar company in St. Louis when the Civil War began, he returned to active duty and became second only to Grant as an important Union commander.

Smith, Andrew Jackson (1815–1897). A Pennsylvanian, after West Point (1838) Smith served in the 1st Dragoons (now the 1st Cavalry) on the frontier, during the Mexican War (briefly commanding the Mormon Battalion), and in the Washington and Oregon territories. In 1861 he briefly commanded the 2nd California Cavalry and was then chief of cavalry under Henry Halleck in the West (1861–1862), rising to brigadier general of volunteers. Smith commanded a division under Sherman in operations against Vicksburg and then a corps in the Red River campaign (March–May 1864). Rising to major general of volunteers, he served in Mississippi (defeating Nathan Bedford Forrest at Tupelo, July 14, 1864), at Nashville (December 15–16, 1864), and in the Mobile campaign (March–April 1865), ending the war with brevets for brigadier general and major general in the regular army. After the war he served as colonel of the 7th Cavalry but resigned in 1869 to become postmaster of St. Louis and a brigadier general in the Missouri militia. He formally retired from the regular army in 1889. He is an officer much in need of a biography.

Smith, James Webster (1850–1876). Born enslaved, after the Civil War Smith attended a Freedman's Bureau school in South Carolina and then Hartford Public High School, in Connecticut. Graduating with honors in 1870, he briefly enrolled in Howard University, but was shortly admitted to West Point, the first African American to attend the Academy. Shunned by white cadets, and under almost continuous harassment by faculty and fellow cadets, including occasional encounters with Fred Grant, Smith was thrice court martialed for supposed infractions, which caused him to be suspended for a year. In 1874, found deficient in philosophy, Smith was dismissed. Shortly afterwards he became a mathematics and military science instructor at the State Agricultural College & Mechanics Institute (now South Carolina State University), and commandant of the school's cadet corps, but died of tuberculosis. In 1997, at the urging of South Carolina's congressional delegation, including notorious segregationist Strom Thurmond, Smith was posthumously commissioned a second lieutenant in the U.S. Army.[16]

---

16 There are brief references to Smith in several books about African Americans at West Point, but it appears there is no biography. See Richard Reid, "Breaking Ground: State College Professor was First Black Enrolled at West Point," *The Times and Democrat* (Orangeburg, SC), June 10, 2012.

Smith, John Eugene (1816–1897). Swiss-born, but raised and educated in Philadelphia, where he became a jeweler, Smith later settled in Galena, Illinois. Early in the war he served as an aide-de-camp to Illinois Governor Richard Yates, and was commissioned colonel of the 45th Illinois Volunteers, mustering into service in December 1861. He led the regiment at Fort Henry, Fort Donelson, Shiloh, Corinth, and in garrison, until November 1862. Promoted to brigadier general of volunteers, he commanded a brigade during the Vicksburg campaign and then a division in the Chattanooga campaign (notably at Missionary Ridge), the Atlanta campaign, the March to the Sea, and the Carolinas campaign. Ending the war with a brevet for major general, Smith entered the regular army as colonel of the newly formed 27th Infantry Regiment, which was later disbanded. Promoted to brigadier general in 1867, he was breveted major general and retired in 1881.

Spaids, Commodore C. (1842–1914). Spaids was a sergeant in Co. A, 4th Illinois Cavalry, Grant's escort company. He mustered into service with the regiment on September 26, 1861, as a corporal, rose to sergeant, and on June 3, 1863, was commissioned second lieutenant. In January 1864 he became a captain in the 1st Mississippi Cavalry, African Descent (3rd U.S. Colored Cavalry). After mustering out Jan 15, 1865, he became a postal worker in Chicago. The name is sometimes found as "Spaides" or "Spaid."[17]

Steele, Frederick (1819–1868). Born in New York, Steele graduated from West Point in 1841, served in the 2nd Infantry in Mexico (two brevets) and in the Yuma War (1850–1853), rising to captain. In May 1861 he became a major in the newly formed regular army 11th Infantry, fought at Wilson's Creek, then became colonel of the 3rd Iowa, campaigning in Missouri. Appointed brigadier general of volunteers in January 1862, Steele commanded a district in Missouri, then a division, fighting at Chickasaw Bayou and Arkansas Post. Promoted to major general of volunteers in March 1863, his division became part of Sherman's Fifteenth Army Corps during the Vicksburg campaign. He then commanded the Army of Arkansas, defeating Kirby Smith and Sterling Price, then a provisional corps which included an African American division during the Mobile campaign, ending the war with brevets to colonel, brigadier general, and major general in the regular army. After the war Steele commanded U.S. troops in Texas to pressure the French out of Mexico, then became colonel of the 20th Infantry, but soon died of a stroke.

Thomas, Lorenzo (1804–1875). An 1824 West Point graduate, Thomas served in the infantry in the Seminole and Mexican Wars and was chief-of-staff

---

17 P. O. Avery, *History of the Fourth Illinois Cavalry Regiment* (Humboldt, NE, 1903), 5–6; Grant, *Papers*, vol. 8, 508.

Maj. Gen. Frederick Steele commanded a division in the Fifteenth Army Corps.
*Library of Congress*

to general-in-chief Winfield Scott, 1853–1861. Lincoln promoted him to colonel and adjutant general of the army, in which post he served almost continuously until 1869. In 1863–1865 he was appointed to recruit Black troops in the Mississippi Valley. Despite having been a slave owner, he became a strong proponent of African American military service and also developed a program that enabled newly freed people to work for wages on plantations managed under military supervision. After the war he became embroiled in the dispute between President Andrew Johnson, whom he supported, and the Republican Congress, and retired from the army in 1869 as a brigadier general and brevet major general.

Tuttle, James Madison (1823–1892). An Indiana businessman and politician, in April 1861 Tuttle raised a company for the 2nd Iowa Infantry, was elected lieutenant colonel, and rose to colonel. He led the regiment ably at Ft. Donelson, then led a brigade at Shiloh, and briefly commanded a division, earning a promotion to brigadier general. From autumn 1862 to spring 1863, he commanded the vital base at Cairo, Illinois. Given a division in Sherman's Fifteenth Army Corps, he led it with distinction in the Vicksburg campaign, then ran unsuccessfully for governor of Iowa. On occupation duty at Natchez, Mississippi, in 1864, he meddled in religious affairs, trying to curb pro-Confederate preachers, and was curbed by Lincoln. Resigning from the army in September 1864, he returned to business and politics in Iowa.

Washburne, Elihu B (1816–1887). Washburne was born in Maine. At the age of 14, to escape poverty, Washburne settled in Galena, Illinois. He managed to get an education, read law, and was elected to the House of Representatives in 1852. On the outbreak of the Civil War his influence enabled his friend, U.S. Grant, to secure a commission in the state militia, and then appointment as a brigadier general in the volunteer army. He remained Grant's life-long political ally. During Grant's presidency he was briefly secretary of state, then served as U.S. minister to France.

Wilson, James Harrison (1837–1925). A native of Illinois, Wilson graduated sixth in his class at West Point in 1860. Commissioned in the Topographical Engineers, he served in the Port Royal expedition, and the battles of Fort Pulaski, South Mountain, and Antietam. Moving west, as a lieutenant colonel he served as inspector general of Grant's Army of the Tennessee for the Vicksburg campaign, then, as a brigadier general, at Chattanooga and Knoxville. Transferring to the cavalry, he became one of the most notable troopers of the war. After the war he worked in engineering, returning to active duty for the Spanish-American War and Boxer Expedition, and retired as a major general.

# APPENDIX II

# PLACES MENTIONED IN THE TEXT

Population Note: Most of the towns and villages mentioned by Fred Grant were quite small, and the numbers of residents are elusive. Where figures are given they are based on the 1860 Census. By 1863, however, wartime pressures would have changed the population of some places dramatically.

Baton Rouge, about 100 miles north of New Orleans, and 150 or so miles south of Vicksburg, then as now the capital of Louisiana, had nearly 5,500 residents. Occupied by Union forces in the spring of 1862, it remained in Union hands until the end of the war.

Bruinsburg, just south of the confluence of the Mississippi with Bayou Pierre, about a dozen miles south of Grand Gulf, was a river port, now lost to the meanderings of the river.

Cairo, in southernmost Illinois, on the peninsula formed by the merger of the Ohio River into the Mississippi, was the terminus of the Illinois Central Rail Road. In 1860 a dismal place with about 2,000 residents, it expanded rapidly during the war, quickly becoming the Union's main base on the Mississippi. All of Grant's operations against Vicksburg were supplied from Cairo (pronounced liked the syrup, Karo).

Carthage, see New Carthage.

De Soto, a small Louisiana town (a short main street and two or three cross streets), on the west side of the peninsula of that name formed by a very sharp bend in the Mississippi, right across the river from Vicksburg. It was the terminus of the Vicksburg and Texas Rail Road.

Dillon's Plantation was about seven miles west of Raymond.

Disharoon's or Di Sharoon's plantation, was on a levee on the west bank of the Mississippi, in Tensas Parish, Louisiana, about 6½ miles southwest of Grand Gulf. Captured by McClernand's corps on April 29th, Grant and his party arrived there shortly before nightfall.

Edward's Station was a small plantation stop on the rail line between Vicksburg (c. 12–13 miles west) and Jackson (c. 25 miles to the east).

Grand Gulf, on the left bank of the Mississippi about 25 miles south of Vicksburg, had once been an important river port with over 1,000 residents. Plagued by yellow fever epidemics and river floods, by 1860 it was virtually abandoned, with fewer than 160 residents. What was left was destroyed during the Vicksburg campaign, and the site is now well inland from the river.

[The] Great Cut at Yazoo Pass was a passage between the Mississippi River and Moon Lake, which provided access to the Yazoo River, the site of an unsuccessful effort by Grant and Rear Adm. David D. Porter in February and March of 1863 to use the connecting waterways to get an army behind Vicksburg.

Greenville, Mississippi, was a very small town on the east bank of the Mississippi, some 90 miles north of Vicksburg by river. Though destroyed by Union troops in 1862, the location, about 125 feet above the river, at a particularly convoluted bend in the stream, remained ideal for artillery to shell passing river traffic, and occasionally Confederate batteries were posted there. The site was raided by Union forces about ten times during the Vicksburg campaign.[1]

Haines or Haynes Bluff, nearly eleven miles north of Vicksburg on the Yazoo River, is more or less the northern portion of Chickasaw Bluffs and was heavily fortified. Confederate troops holding the bluff were withdrawn into Vicksburg about May 20th, when Grant began the siege of the city.

Hard Times, a Louisiana plantation located on the river, some three miles across the Mississippi from Grand Gulf, is now lost to the shifting of the river.

Helena, Arkansas, a river port on the west bank of the Mississippi, with about 1,100 inhabitants, was the seat of a major cotton growing county, in which enslaved African Americans comprised about 60 percent of the 14,000 or so residents. Captured by the Union in August 1862, it was heavily fortified. On July 4, 1863, Confederate forces unsuccessfully attacked the place, in a very belated attempt to relieve pressure on Vicksburg.

---

1 See, for example, *O.R.* XIII, 240*ff*; *O.R.* XXIV, pt. 1, 2, 3, 4; and *O.R.* XXIV, pt. 3, 158, where Sherman, writing on March 31, 1863, noted "Greenville has been a favorite point from which to assail our passing boats" before ordering another raid. It was shortly occupied by a division, to cover the northern flank of the forces besieging Vicksburg. See also Daniel R. Doyle, "The Civil War in the Greenville Bends," *The Arkansas Historical Quarterly* 70, no. 2 (Summer 2011): 131–161.

Jackson, the Mississippi state capital, about 45 miles east of Vicksburg, had about 3,200 residents, nearly 1,800 in slavery, with only about a dozen free Black people.

Milliken's Bend, Louisiana, a small steamboat port two or three miles above Young's Point on the Mississippi, about 15 miles upstream from Vicksburg, had about 200 inhabitants in 1860, many enslaved. It became a major Union supply depot, now lost to the whims of the river. On the major action there by the US Colored Troops in June 1863, see page 60, note 4.

New Carthage, Louisiana, a village of about four streets wide on the Louisiana side of the Mississippi, some 20 miles downstream from Vicksburg, now lost to the shifting of the river.

Port Gibson, Mississippi, a river port about 30 miles south of Vicksburg, is situated on a 118-foot-high ridge and had about 1,450 residents, including about 560 African Americans, all but about two dozen held in slavery.

Port Hudson, Louisiana, a river town about 25 miles upriver from Baton Rouge, and 130 or so south of Vicksburg, is on a bluff 80 feet above a tight bend in the Mississippi. Already in decline by 1862 with only a few hundred inhabitants, it was heavily fortified after the fall of New Orleans. With Vicksburg on the north, it anchored the southern end of the last stretch of the Mississippi controlled by the Confederacy. Besieged by some 40,000 Union troops under Maj. Gen. Nathaniel Banks in May, the 7,000-strong garrison surrendered a few days after the fall of Vicksburg; Union casualties from disease were very heavy.[2]

Raymond, Mississippi was a small town about 36 miles east of Vicksburg, 18 or 20 miles west of Jackson. It had about 560 inhabitants, including some 225 African Americans, all but seven enslaved.

Richmond was a Louisiana settlement about five miles south of Milliken's Bend and seven miles southwest of Young's Point.

Rodney was a small town of fewer than 200 people, about a dozen miles south of Port Gibson. Once near the Mississippi, now it is well away from it.

Vicksburg, a major river port about 250 miles north of New Orleans, had about 4,600 residents in 1860, a third enslaved, with fewer than three dozen free African Americans. The population soared as Grant's army approached. Sitting on a ridge high above a significant bend in the river, it was the most defensible position on the Mississippi, and heavily fortified, with some four miles of works on its river front and over six miles on the landward side by the time Grant's army began the siege.

---

2 Lawrence Lee Hewitt, *Port Hudson, Confederate Bastion on the Mississippi* (Baton Rouge, 1987).

Warrenton, Mississippi was a small port on the Mississippi, about six miles south of Vicksburg. Once the county seat, it was eclipsed by Vicksburg and heavily fortified by the Confederates. It is now well inland from the river.

Young's Point was a bend in the Mississippi on the Louisiana side, about eight miles upstream from Vicksburg, near Milliken's Bend. Occupied in force by Union troops in January of 1863, Grant had his headquarters there for a time, and by the end of March it was a major Union base.

# Appendix III

# Order of Battle

## THE VICKSBURG CAMPAIGN
## MARCH 29–JULY 4, 1863[1]

Unites States Order of Battle

Army of the Tennessee
Maj. Gen. Ulysses S. Grant, commanding[2]

Acting Inspector General
Brig. Gen. Jeremiah C. Sullivan

Chief of Staff
Lt. Col. John A. Rawlins

Chief of Transportation
Col. Joseph D. Webster

Ninth Army Corps
Maj. Gen. John Parke, arrived mid-June

First Division
Brig. Gen. Thomas Welsh

---

1 Christopher Gabel, *Staff Ride Handbook For The Vicksburg Campaign, December 1862–July 1863* (Fort Leavenworth, KS, 2015), 164–173; Kevin Dougherty, *The Vicksburg Campaign: Strategy, Battles and Key Figures* (Jefferson, NC, 2015); Smith, *The Siege of Vicksburg*, 535–563. *Note*: In the 19th century, the U.S. Army wrote out corps and division numbers, rather than indicate them with Roman or Arabic numerals.

2 Beginning with about 45,000 troops in early April, Grant's army was gradually reinforced, so that by the surrender of Vicksburg he had some 74,000–75,000 active personnel, despite casualties of about 9,000. Not all of these formations were actively engaged in the siege of Vicksburg; some were securing Grant's lines of supply or guarding against potential attempts by Confederate forces to relieve the city.

Second Division
Brig. Gen. Robert B. Potter

Thirteenth Army Corps
Maj. Gen. John A. McClernand, replaced by
Maj. Gen. Edward O. C. Ord, in mid-June 1863

Ninth Division
Brig. Gen. Peter J. Osterhaus

Tenth Division
Brig. Gen. Andrew J. Smith

Twelfth Division
Brig. Gen. Alvin P. Hovey

Fourteenth Division
Brig. Gen. Eugene A. Carr

Fifteenth Army Corps
Maj. Gen. William T. Sherman

First Division
Maj. Gen. Frederick Steele

Second Division
Maj. Gen. Francis Preston Blair Jr.

Third Division
Brig. Gen. James M. Tuttle

Sixteenth Army Corps [Partial Detachment]
Maj. Gen. Cadwallader C. Washburn

First Division
Brig. Gen. William Sooy Smith, arrived June 12

Fourth Division
Brig. Gen. Jacob G. Lauman, arrived May 13

Provisional Division
Brig. Gen. Nathan Kimball, arrived June 3

Seventeenth Army Corps
Maj. Gen. James B. McPherson

Third Division
Maj. Gen. John A. Logan

Sixth Division
Brig. Gen. John McArthur

Seventh Division
Brig. Gen. Isaac Quinby, replaced by
Brig. Gen. John E. Smith, June 3

Herron's Division
Maj. Gen. Francis J. Herron, arrived June 11

Detachment, District of Northeast Louisiana
Brig. Gen. Elias S. Dennis

Confederate Order of Battle[3]

Army of Mississippi or Army of Vicksburg
Lt. Gen. John C. Pemberton, commanding[4]

Loring's Division
Maj. Gen. William W. Loring[5]

Stevenson's Division
Maj. Gen. Carter L. Stevenson

Forney's Division
Maj. Gen. John H. Forney

Smith's Division
Maj. Gen. Martin L. Smith

Bowen's Division
Maj. Gen. John S. Bowen

River Batteries
Col. Edward Higgins[6]

3  Confederate practice customarily referred to military formations by the names of their commanders.

4  By the beginning of April, Pemberton had about 43,000–45,000 troops but lost about 9,000 after they were cut off from his army by Union forces, ending up under Gen. Joseph E. Johnston's command. Casualties during the campaign and siege seem to have amounted to about 8,000 or so, as only about 30,000 troops surrendered, including many wounded.

5  Loring and his division were separated from the army after its defeat at Champion Hill, May 16, 1863, and joined Johnston's relief force slowly gathering east of Vicksburg, which threatened, but never actually fell on Grant's rear during the siege.

6  Higgins commanded the artillery overlooking the Mississippi riverfront.

# APPENDIX IV

# "OLD SHADY"[1]

On May 24, 1861, at Fort Monroe on the tip of the Virginia Peninsula, Maj. Gen. Benjamin Butler refused to return three fugitives from slavery to their enslaver, asserting that they were "contraband of war," a term usually referring to goods that are of military value, and thus subject to confiscation. "Contraband" quickly became a popular term for escaped slaves. Some musicians began writing songs around the theme of "contraband." One such was Benjamin Russel Hanby

1 Society of the Army of the Tennessee, *Report of the Proceedings of the Society of the Army of the Tennessee at the Sixth Annual Meeting, Held at Madison, Wisconsin, July 3rd and 4th 1872* (Cincinnati, 1877), 249, 386, 414, 521; Society of the Army of the Tennessee, *Report of the Proceedings of the Society of the Army of the Tennessee at the Fourteenth Annual Meeting, Held at Cincinnati, Ohio, April 6th and 7th 1881* (Cincinnati, 1885), 34, 165, 177–178, 377, 525, 544–545; W. T. Sherman, "Old Shady, with a Moral," The North American Review 147, no. 383 (Oct., 1888): 361–368; Keith P. Wilson and Keith Malcolm Wilson, *Campfires of Freedom: The Camp Life of Black Soldiers During the Civil War* (Kent, OH, 2002), 151–152; Michael C. Cohen, *The Social Lives of Poems in Nineteenth-Century America* (Philadelphia, 2015), 121–123; "Stephen T. Gordon," Brass Net, https://www.brasshistory.net/Gordon%20History.pdf, accessed Oct. 24, 2021; Clement A. Lounsberry, "Blakely Durant, The Composer and Original Singer of one of Our Most Popular and Stirring War Songs," *History of North Dakota* (Chicago,1917), 1:496–498; "An Old Camp Minstrel," The Princeton (Minnesota) Union, May 25, 1893, 8; C. M. Hartwick, "'Old Shady,' the Composer and Original Singer of One of Our Most Stirring and Popular War Songs," *The Midland Monthly Magazine* 11, no. 6 (Dec. 1894): 454–456; "'Old Shady': Civil War Vet Who Died in GF was Cook for Gen. Sherman," *Grand Forks Herald*, April 28, 2011, online at https://www.grandforksherald.com/2153610-old-shady-civil-war-vet-who-died-gf-was-cook-gen-sherman, accessed Aug. 28, 2021; Arnold P. Powers, *Devour Us Not: Short Stories from African-American History* (2013), 112; C. B. Galbreath "Song Writers of Ohio: Benjamin Russel Hanby, Author of 'Darling Nelly Gray,'" *Ohio History Journal* 14, no. 2 (April 1905): 196–197; Cohen, *The Social Lives of Poems in Nineteenth-Century America*, 121–123, which discusses the lyrics, not the tune or its origin.

(1833–1867), who had already produced one popular tune, "Darling Nellie Gray" (1856). In 1861 Oliver Ditson & Co. of Boston published Hanby's "Ole Shady, or the Song of the Contraband."[2] Dedicated to General Butler, the lyrics (reproduced below) were a light-hearted account in what at the time passed for African American dialect of a slave who is leaving Jefferson Davis and company to join his family in Canada.

Enter, D. Blakely Durant (1826–1894), an African American cook who served Federal troops in the west from 1862 through 1863. A freeborn man, not an escaped slave, like the "Ole Shady" of the song, Durant seems to have acquired the nickname "Old Shady" because he would sometimes play guitar and sing, and often sang Hanby's "Ole Shady."[3] Durant helped popularize the song, to the point that the Supervisory Committee for Recruiting Colored Regiments published the lyrics in a broadside as "A Contraband Song. Old Shady."[4] Though the broadside attributed the words to a "contraband genius," there are only minimal differences between the broadside and Hanby's lyrics.

Because there was no easy way to communicate new tunes (one would have to either hear it performed or be able to read music), it was common in the nineteenth century to suggest an already familiar tune to which the lyrics could be sung. The broadside specified "Away Down South" as the "air," which was an 1848 minstrel song "written and composed" by Stephen Foster (1826–1864). It is unknown whether Durant performed "Ole Shady" using Foster's or Hanby's tune.

A tune Durant did *not* use is that composed by David A. Warden (1820–1890), since the latter (entitled "Old Shady Contraband Song and Chorus") was not published until 1864 (by S. T. Gordon in New York). Warden largely repeated Hanby's lyrics but added a third "coming" to the chorus, presumably to better fit Warden's music.

Many people who heard Durant perform "Ole Shady" (including General Sherman) simply assumed that Durant wrote the song.[5] Hanby's widow quickly

---

2  Posted at www.loc.gov, accessed Feb. 17, 2022.

3  Fred Grant described one such performance that took place on April 22, 1863. Frederick D. Grant, "The Lincoln Banquet at the Abraham Lincoln Centre," *Unity*, Feb. 25, 1909, 404. "An Old Camp Minstrel," *The Princeton* (Minnesota) *Union*, May 25, 1893, calls "Old Shady" Grant's favorite song; but then also inaccurately reports that Durant was a contraband.

4  The Supervisory Committee for Recruiting Colored Regiments promoted recruiting of African Americans with posters and songs, and operated schools for men seeking to become officers in the USCT.

5  W. T. Sherman, "Old Shady, with a Moral," *The North American Review* 147, no. 383 (Oct. 1888), 361–368.

set Sherman straight, but Sherman's misattribution has received more play than his retraction.[6]

Hanby produced another song whose popularity endured well into the twentieth century: "Santa Claus" (first line, "Up on the rooftop reindeer pause"), written in 1864 and published in 1866. As for "Old Shady," the *song* remained popular at reunions of the Federal Army of Tennessee, while the man retired to Grand Forks, North Dakota.[7]

"Ole Shady, [or]
The Song of the Contraband"

1. Oh Yah! yah! darkies, laugh wid me,
For de white folks say Ole Shady's free,
So dont you see dat de jubilee
Is a coming, coming, Hail! mighty day.

CHORUS [sung after each verse]
Den away, away for I can't wait any longer,
Hooray, I'm going home
[Repeat the two lines]

2. Oh Mass' got scared and so did his lady
Dis chile breaks for Ole Uncle Aby,
"Open de gates! out here's ole Shady
A coming, coming," Hail mighty day.

3. Good bye, Mass' Jeff, good bye Mis'r Stephens,[8]
'Scuse dis niggah for takin his leavins,

6  C. B. Galbreath "Song Writers of Ohio: Benjamin Russel Hanby, Author of 'Darling Nelly Gray,'" *Ohio History Journal* 14, no.2 (April 1905): 196–197; C. M. Hartwick, "'Old Shady,' the Composer and Original Singer of One of Our Most Stirring and Popular War Songs," *The Midland Monthly Magazine* 1, no. 6 (Dec. 1894): 454–456; Clement A. Lounsberry, "Blakely Durant," *History of North Dakota* I:496–498; Wilson and Wilson, *Campfires of Freedom*, 151–152. An account that discusses both sides of the issue is "'Old Shady': Civil War Vet Who Died in GF was Cook for Gen. Sherman," *Grand Forks Herald*, April 28, 2011, online at https://www.grandforksherald.com/2153610-old-shady-civil-war-vet-who-died-gf-was-cook-gen-sherman, accessed Feb. 17, 2022.

7  Society of the Army of the Tennessee, *Report of the Proceedings of the Society of the Army of the Tennessee at the Sixth Annual Meeting*, 249, 386, 414, 521; Society of the Army of the Tennessee, *Report of the Proceedings of the Society of the Army of the Tennessee at the Fourteenth Annual Meeting*, 34, 165, 177–178, 377, 525, 544–545.

8  The references are to Jefferson F. Davis, Confederate president, and Alexander Stephens, Davis's vice president.

'Spect, pretty soon you'll hear uncle Abram's.
Coming, coming, Hail mighty day.

4. Good bye hard work wid never any pay,
I'se a gwine up North where the good folks say
Dat white wheat bread and a dollar a day.
Are a coming, coming, Hail mighty day.

5. Oh, I've got a wife, and I've got a baby,
Living up yonder in Lower Canady,
Wont dey laugh when dey see ole Shady,
Coming, coming, Hail mighty day.

# THE GRAND ARMY OF THE REPUBLIC AND THE NATIONAL TRIBUNE

Formed in 1866 at Springfield, Illinois, the Grand Army of the Republic (GAR) was open to any Union military veteran of the Civil War. Its membership included all races and creeds, including some women who had served. The GAR was organized into hundreds of "posts," which existed in every state, though most of them were in the North, and a few abroad.

The GAR was the first, and most important, veterans' advocacy group in the United States, supporting better pensions, survivor's benefits, the establishment of old soldiers' homes, and promoting memorialization of the war and the veteran, as well as the annual observation of "Decoration Day" (now known as "Memorial Day"), and staunchly endorsing Republican candidates.[1]

Membership in the GAR peaked at 427,981 in 1890, nearly a quarter of all who had served the Union during the war, and almost 40 percent of the 1,099,668 living veterans.[2]

Because the GAR limited membership to veterans of the Civil War—flatly refusing to alter its policy when veterans of the wars with Spain and in the Philippines asked to join—it began to lose influence as its membership died off

---

1   For the GAR see Stuart McConnell, *Glorious Contentment: The Grand Army of the Republic, 1865–1900* (Chapel Hill, NC, 1997); Barbara A. Gannon, *The Won Cause: Black and White Comradeship in the Grand Army of the Republic* (Chapel Hill, 2011); Brian Matthew Jordan, *Marching Home: Union Veterans and Their Unending Civil War* (New York, 2015).

2   Kellee Blake, "'First in the Path of the Firemen': The Fate of the 1890 Population Census, Part 2," *Prologue Magazine* 28, no 1 (Spring 1996), https://www.archives.gov/publications/prologue/1996/spring/1890-census-2.html, accessed Nov. 4, 2021.

and newer veterans' organizations began forming. The GAR formally dissolved on the death of the last Union veteran, Albert Woolson, in 1956.

In 1877 George E. Lemon of Washington, D.C., began publishing the *National Tribune*, a monthly newspaper that described itself as "devoted to the interests of the Soldiers and Sailors of the late war, and all Pensioners of the United States." It soon became a weekly and was a major organ for the GAR.[3] The paper's normal fare ran to articles supporting veterans' pension rights, including, at times, transcripts of endlessly tedious congressional debates, liberally seasoned with equally dull notices of applications by local veterans' groups for charters as GAR posts. More interesting are the obituaries of veterans and other persons with some connection to the war or veterans' affairs. There were also veterans' reminiscences and tales of derring-do in the late war, occasional inquiries by veterans seeking old comrades or attempting to clear up some obscure point about the war, and some humorous pieces on military life. The paper also had a "Women's Department" for the wives and daughters of the veterans.

From time to the time, the *National Tribune* showed a spark of brilliance, for example in 1881 it held a "contest" to determine who had been the youngest soldier in the war, which elicited numerous letters, most making bogus or second-hand claims, with the net result that circulation stayed high while no real conclusion was reached.

The fate of the *National Tribune* was, of course, closely tied to that of the GAR, and as membership in the veterans' organization rose the paper's circulation may have reached 250,000, before declining and going out of business in 1917.

Materials that appeared in the *National Tribune* can often be of some interest to the historian, such as veteran's inquiries seeking to clarify a particular incident or offering anecdotes about their wartime experiences. In addition, several memoirs were serialized in the paper, such as those of Brig. Gen. William Passmore Carlin, which ran to about 30,000 words in 20 installments. Among those memoirs was one that began on January 20, 1887, with the publication of the first of Fred's four-part, 18,000-word "General Ulysses S. Grant: His Son's Memories of Him in the Field," found in Section I.

---

3  Albert A. Nofi, "The Battle of Podunksburg," *North & South* 9, Series I, no. 4 (Aug. 2006): 94*ff*.

# Appendix VI

# Some Civil War Military Terminology

Since some 19th century military terms may be unfamiliar to modern readers, some brief definitions are given here.

Adjutant / Adjutant General: The principal administrative officer of a regiment or larger formation, serving under the commander, and also the title of the senior-most administrative officer of a state's military forces or of the US Army or of a major military formation, such as the Army of the Tennessee.

Aide-de-camp: An officer assigned as an assistant to a senior officer, such as a general. Often found as "aide."

Brevet: Essentially an honorary rank, usually awarded for outstanding courage or services. A brevet conferred prestige on an officer, making him technically senior to another officer of equal rank under certain circumstances, such as at the direction of the president, or when assigned to court-martial duty or command of a special detail, during which the officer would receive the appropriate higher pay. Bearers of brevets were often addressed in their higher honorary rank, which can sometimes be confusing; for example, during the Vicksburg campaign U. S. Grant was a former captain in the regular army, serving as a major general of volunteers. He was promoted to major general in the regular army as of July 4, 1863, the surrender of Vicksburg.

Chief-of-staff: A senior military commander's principal subordinate, who coordinates the various staff departments, develops plans for the commander's approval, and so forth.

Battery Powell, a series of "V" shaped gun emplacements, one of the many works erected by
Grant's army during the siege of Vicksburg, from a sketch by Theodore R. Davis.
*Harper's Weekly*

Muster in /muster out: The formal acceptance of an organization or individual for federal service, and the formal discharge of an organization or individual from such service.

Provost Marshal: The officer in charge of military police.

## SIEGE TERMINOLOGY

Approaches: Trenches dug toward the enemy defenses in a zigzag fashion, linking parallels.

Lunet: More correctly "Lunette," a V-shaped defensive work with the back open, used for emplacing artillery.

Mines: Tunnels dug under an enemy's defenses, which can be filled with explosives and detonated to blow up the works. The defender may attempt counter-mining, to locate and block the attacker's mines, at times leading to bloody underground battles in the dark.

Parallels: A series of trench lines literally parallel to the enemy defenses, connected to each other and to the rear by approaches. As a line of parallels is finished, approaches can be pushed closer to the enemy in zig-zag fashion, permitting another line of parallels to be constructed. This process can be repeated until the final parallel—usually the third—is near enough to the enemy defenses to mount an assault or emplace cannon to fire into the enemy defenses.

Redan: A stand-alone V-shaped earthen or masonry bastion, or a similarly shaped part of a fort or extensive field works.

Regular Army/Volunteer Army/militia: The "Regular Army" was the permanent force of the United States. The "Volunteer Army" comprised forces raised by states specifically for federal service during the war. For officers, the distinction between regulars and volunteers was particularly important, because a regular officer could hold a volunteer rank higher than his permanent regular army rank, to which he would return upon being discharged from the volunteer army. The "militia" were the armed citizen forces of the states, sometimes temporarily committed to the field, often in emergencies or to hold fortifications. On paper an officer could hold rank in all three services and would often be referred to by whichever rank was the highest, which can cause some confusion.

# BIBLIOGRAPHY

Grant Family Writings

Grant, Frederick D. "A Boy's Experience at Vicksburg." *Personal Recollections of the War of the Rebellion, Addresses Delivered before the Commandery of the State of New York Military Order of the Loyal Legion of the United States.* Edited by A. Noel Blakeman. New York: G. P. Putnam's, 1907. 86–100.

———. "Annual Address." *Report of the Proceedings of the Society of the Army of the Tennessee at the Thirty-Seventh Meeting, Held at Vicksburg, Mississippi, November 7–8, 1907.* Cincinnati: Charles L. Ebel, 1908. 95-122.

———. "General Fred Grant's Scare at Vicksburg." *Literary Digest* 44, no. 17 (April 27, 1912), 898–902.

———. "Fred Grant as a Boy with the Army." *Confederate Veteran* XVI, no. 1 (Jan. 1908).

———. "General Grant as a Father," *Youth's Companion* 73, no. 3 (Jan. 19, 1899) 1–6.

———. "General Ulysses S. Grant: His Son's Memories of Him in the Field—Part I." *National Tribune,* Jan. 20, 1887.

———. "General Ulysses S. Grant: His Son's Memories of Him in the Field—Part II." *National Tribune,* Jan. 27, 1887.

———. "General Ulysses S. Grant: His Son's Memories of Him in the Field—Part III." *National Tribune,* Feb. 3, 1887.

———. "General Ulysses S. Grant: His Son's Memories of Him in the Field—Part IV." *National Tribune,* Feb. 10, 1887.

———. "The Lincoln Banquet at the Abraham Lincoln Centre." *Unity,* Feb. 25, 1909, 404*ff.*

———. "Oration." *Report of the Proceedings of the Society at the Twenty-Seventh Meeting, held in Cincinnati, O., and Chattanooga, Tenn., September 16–21, 1895.* Cincinnati: F. W. Freeman, 1896.

———. "Reminiscences of General U. S. Grant, Read Before the Illinois Commandery of the Loyal Legion of the United States, January 27, 1910." *Journal of the Illinois State Historical Society* VII, no.1 (April 1914), 72–76.

———. *"With Grant at Vicksburg." The Outlook* 59, no. 9. (July 2, 1898): 533–543.

Grant, Julia Dent. *The Personal Memoirs of Julia Dent Grant (Mrs. Ulysses S. Grant).* Edited by John Y. Simon. New York: Putnam, 1975.

Grant, Ulysses S., *Letters of U. S. Grant to His Father and Younger Sister, 1857–1878.* Edited by Jesse Grant Cramer. New York: G. P. Putnam's, 1912.

———. *The Papers of Ulysses S. Grant.* Edited by John Y. Simon, et al. Carbondale: Southern Illinois University, 1969–2012. 32 volumes.

————. *Personal Memoirs of U. S. Grant.* New York: Charles L. Webster, 1885. Two volumes.

————. *The Personal Memoirs of Ulysses S. Grant: The Complete Annotated Edition.* Edited by John F. Marszalek with David S. Nolen & Louie P. Gallo. Cambridge, Massachusetts: The Belknap Press of Harvard University Press, 2017.

## Fred Grant Interviews

Carpenter, Frank G. "A Chat with Fred Grant." *St. Louis Republic,* Aug. 21, 1904.

Morrow, James B. "General Frederick Dent Grant, Recollections of his Famous Father." *The Ulysses S. Grant Association Newsletter* 9, no. 2 (January 1972): 1–14.

"Reminiscences of General Frederick Dent Grant." *The Ulysses S. Grant Association Newsletter* 6, no. 3 (April 1969): 1–23. Reprinted from *The New York World Sunday Magazine,* April 25, 1897.

Watrous, A. E. "Grant as His Son Saw Him: An Interview With Colonel Frederick D. Grant About His Father." *McClure's Magazine* II, no. 6 (May 1894): 515–519.

## Memoirs and Regimental Histories

Avery, P. O. *History of the Fourth Illinois Cavalry Regiment.* Humboldt, NE: The Enterprise, 1903.

Bartlett, Napier. *A Soldier's Story of the War: Including the Marches and Battles of the Washington Artillery and of Other Louisiana Troops.* New Orleans: Clark & Hofeline, 1873.

Brown, Alonzo L. *History of the Fourth Regiment of Minnesota Infantry Volunteers during the Great Rebellion, 1861–1865.* St. Paul, MN: The Pioneer Press, 1892.

Cadwallader, Sylvanus. *Three Years with Grant, As Recalled by War Correspondent Sylvanus Cadwallader.* Edited by Benjamin P. Thomas. New York: Knopf, 1955.

Dana, Charles A. *Recollections of the Civil War: With Leaders at Washington and in the Field in the Sixties.* New York: D. Appleton, 1899.

Evans, John Davis. *Silencing the Vicksburg Guns: The Story of the 7th Missouri Infantry Regiment as Experienced by John Davis Evans, Union Private and Mormon Pioneer.* Edited by Jerry Evan Crouch. Victoria, BC: Trafford Publishing, 2005.

McKinley, Emilie Riley. *From the Pen of a She-Rebel: The Civil War Diary of Emilie Riley McKinley.* Edited by Gordon A. Cotton. Columbia: University of South Carolina Press, 2001.

Owen, William M. *In Camp and Battle with the Washington Artillery of New Orleans.* Baton Rouge: Louisiana State University, 1999.

Sherman, William T. *Memoirs of General William T. Sherman.* New York: D. Appleton, 1886. Two volumes.

Porter, David Dixon. *Anecdotes and Incidents of the Civil War.* New York: D. Appleton, 1885.

————. *The Naval History of the Civil War.* New York: Sherman Publishing Company, 1886.

Porter, Horace, *Campaigning with Grant.* New York: The Century Co., 1897.

*The Story of the Fifty-fifth Regiment Illinois Volunteer Infantry in the Civil War, 1861–1865.* Clinton, MA: W. J. Coulter, 1887.

## Official Documents and Reference Works

Allardice, Bruce S. *Confederate Colonels, A Biographical Dictionary.* Columbus: University of Missouri Press, 2008.

Cullum, George W. *Biographical Register of the Officers and Graduates of the United States Military Academy at West Point, New York, Since its Establishment in 1802.* Boston: Houghton, Mifflin, 1891. Available online at the USMA Library Digital Collection, http://digital-library.usma.edu/digital/collection/p16919coll3/id/13311.

Heitman, Francis R. *Historical Register and Dictionary of the United States Army, From its Organization, September 19, 1789, to March 2, 1903.* Washington, D.C.: Government Printing Office, 1903. Two volumes.

Hunt, Rodger D., and Jack R. Brow. *Brevet Brigadier Generals in Blue.* Gaithersburg, MD: Olde Soldier Books, 1990.

Hunt, Rodger D. *Colonels in Blue.* Various publishers, 2001–2022. Eight volumes.

Mooney, James Longuemare. *The Dictionary of American Naval Fighting Ships.* Washington, D.C.: Navy Dept., Office of the Chief of Naval Operations, Naval History Division, 1959–1991. Nine volumes.

*Official Army Register for 1863.* Washington, D.C.: The Adjutant General's Office, 1863.

*Official Army Register of the Volunteer Force of the United States Army for the Years 1861, '62, '63, '64, '65.* Washington, D.C.: The Adjutant General's Office, 1865. Seven volumes, listing officers only.

*Official Records of the Union and Confederate Armies in the War of the Rebellion.* Washington, D.C.: Government Printing Office, from 1881. 70 volumes in 128 tomes, in three series.

*Official Records of the Union and Confederate Navies in the War of the Rebellion.* Washington, D.C.: Government Printing Office, from 1894. 30 volumes.

*Official Register of the United States, Containing a list of the Officers and Employees in the Civil, Military, and Naval Service.* Washington, D.C.: Government Printing Office, 1905.

Warner, Ezra, *Generals in Blue: Lives of the Union Commanders.* Baton Rouge: Louisiana State University Press, 1964.

———. *Generals in Gray: Lives of the Confederate Commanders.* Baton Rouge: Louisiana State University Press, 1959.

## Newspapers & Periodicals

"The Bridge at Bayou Pierre Loss in Skirmishing." *New York Times*, May 23, 1863.

"An Old Camp Minstrel." *The Princeton* (Minnesota) *Union,* May 25, 1893.

Davis, Theodore. "Grant Under Fire." *The Cosmopolitan: A Monthly Illustrated Magazine* 14, no. 3 (January 1893): 336–337.

De La Cruz, Donna. "Utah Passes 'Free-Range' Parenting Law." *New York Times,* March 29, 2018.

"Gen. Grant's Career." *New York Times,* April 12, 1912.

"Gen. Fred Grant's Battle: The Event of the Week at Chickamauga was the Sham Engagement Under His Direction." *New York Times,* June 26, 1898.

"George W. Barnes." *The Washington Bee,* June 27, 1908.

Hartwick, C. M. "'Old Shady,' the Composer and Original Singer of One of Our Most Stirring and Popular War Songs," *The Midland Monthly Magazine* 11, no. 6 (December 1894): 454–456.

"The Late Colonel Bowers." *Harper's Weekly,* March 24, 1866.

Nelson, Stanley. "Grant & Son on the Mississippi." *Concordia Sentinel,* July 5, 2017.

"Obituary. Henry Stewart Hewit, MD." *The Medical Record.* Sept. 1, 1873.

"Passing in Review at Chickamauga, the New York Regiments Showed Off to Advantage." *New York Times,* June 4, 1898.

Reid, Richard. "Breaking Ground: State College Professor was First Black Enrolled at West Point." *The Times and Democrat* (Orangeburg, SC), June 10, 2012.

"Relic Comes Home." *100 Years After* 3, no. 3 (March 1960).

Richard, J. Fraise. "Grant's Life Saved; Colored Servant in Need." *The Washington Bee,* May 27, 1911.

Sherman, W. T., "Old Shady, with a Moral." *The North American Review* 147, no. 383 (October 1888): 361–368.

## Books & Scholarly Publications

Barnickel, Linda. *Milliken's Bend: A Civil War Battle in History and in Memory.* (Baton Rouge: Louisiana State University Press, 2013).

Bartlett, Napier. *A Soldier's Story of the War: Including the Marches and Battles of the Washington Artillery and of Other Louisiana Troops* (New Orleans: Clark & Hofeline, 1873).

Bearss, Edwin C., with J. Parker Hills. *Receding Tide: Vicksburg and Gettysburg: The Campaigns that Changed the Civil War.* Washington, D.C.: National Geographic Society, 2010.

Bearss, Edwin C., and Warren Grabau. *The Battle of Jackson, May 14, 1863. The Siege of Jackson, July 10–17, 1863. Three Other Post-Vicksburg Actions.* Baltimore: The Jackson Civil War Roundtable, Inc., 1981.

Carter III, Samuel. *The Final Fortress: The Campaign for Vicksburg, 1862–1863.* New York: St. Martin's Press, 1980.

Chernow, Ron. *Grant.* New York: Penguin Press, 2017.

Cohen, Michael C. *The Social Lives of Poems in Nineteenth-Century America.* Philadelphia: University of Pennsylvania Press, 2015.

Cramer, M. J. *Ulysses S. Grant: Conversations and Unpublished Letters.* New York: Eaton & Mains, 1897.

Dougherty, Kevin. *The Vicksburg Campaign: Strategy, Battles and Key Figures.* Jefferson, NC: McFarland, 2015.

Dowdall, Denise M. *From Cincinnati to the Colorado Ranger: The Horsemanship of Ulysses S. Grant.* Dublin: Historyeye, 2012.

Doyle, Daniel R. "The Civil War in the Greenville Bends." *The Arkansas Historical Quarterly* 70, no. 2 (Summer 2011): 131–161.

Dugard, Martin. *The Training Ground: Grant, Lee, Sherman, and Davis in the Mexican War, 1846–1848.* Lincoln: University of Nebraska Press, 2009.

Farina, William. *Ulysses S. Grant, 1861–1864: His Rise from Obscurity to Military Greatness.* Jefferson, NC: McFarland, 2007.

Feis, William B. "Charles S. Bell: Union Scout." *North & South* 4 , no. 5 (June 2001): 26–37.

Gabel, Christopher. *Staff Ride Handbook for the Vicksburg Campaign, December 1862–July 1863.* Fort Leavenworth, KS: Army University Press, 2015.

Galbreath, C. B. "Song Writers of Ohio: Benjamin Russel Hanby, Author of 'Darling Nelly Gray.'" *Ohio History Journal* 14, no. 2 (April 1905).

Gannon, Barbara A. *The Won Cause: Black and White Comradeship in the Grand Army of the Republic.* Chapel Hill: University of North Carolina Press, 2011.

Groom, Winston. *Vicksburg, 1863.* New York: A. A. Knopf, 2009.

Harris, Stephen L. *Duty, Honor, Privilege.* Washington, D.C.: Brassey's, 2001.

Hewitt, Lawrence Lee. *Port Hudson, Confederate Bastion on the Mississippi.* Baton Rouge: Louisiana State University Press, 1987.

Hollandsworth Jr, James G. *Pretense of Glory: The Life of General Nathaniel P. Banks.* Baton Rouge: Louisiana State University Press, 1999,

Jordan, Brian Matthew. *Marching Home: Union Veterans and Their Unending Civil War.* New York: Liveright, 2015.

McConnell, Stuart. *Glorious Contentment: The Grand Army of the Republic, 1865–1900.* Chapel Hill, NC: University of North Carolina Press, 1997.

Miller, Donald L. *Vicksburg: Grant's Campaign that Broke the Confederacy.* New York: Simon & Schuster, 2019.

Miller, Francis Trevelyan, and Robert S. Lanier. *The Photographic History of the Civil War.* New York: The Review of Reviews, 1911.

Miller, Mary Carol. *Lost Landmarks of Mississippi.* Jackson, MS: University Press of Mississippi, 2002.

Longacre, Edward. *General Ulysses S. Grant, the Soldier and the Man.* Philadelphia: Da Capo, 2006.

Lounsberry, Clement A. "Blakely Durant, The Composer and Original Singer of one of Our Most Popular and Stirring War Songs." *History of North Dakota.* Chicago: S. L. Clarke Publishing, 1917.

Nofi, Albert A. "The Battle of Podunksburg." *North & South* 9, Series I, no. 4 (August 2006): 94*ff*.

Powers, Arnold P. *Devour Us Not: Short Stories from African-American History.* X-Libris, 2013.

Reeves, John *Soldier of Destiny: Slavery, Secession, and the Redemption of Ulysses S. Grant* (New York: Pegasus Books, 2023),

Ross, Ishbel. *The General's Wife: The Life of Mrs. Ulysses S. Grant.* New York, Dodd, Mead, 1959.

Simpson, Brooks D. *Ulysses S. Grant: Triumph Over Adversity, 1822–1865.* Boston: Houghton Mifflin, 2000.

Smith, Timothy B. *The Real Horse Soldiers: Benjamin Grierson's Epic 1863 Civil War Raid Through Mississippi.* El Dorado Hills, CA: Savas Beatie, 2018.

———. *The Siege of Vicksburg: Climax of the Campaign to Open the Mississippi River, May 23–July 4, 1863.* Lawrence: University Press of Kansas, 2021.

Society of the Army of the Tennessee, *Report of the Proceedings of the Society of the Army of the Tennessee at the Sixth Annual Meeting, Held at Madison, Wisconsin, July 3rd and 4th 1872.* Cincinnati: The Society, 1877.

———. *Report of the Proceedings of the Society of the Army of the Tennessee at the Fourteenth Annual Meeting, Held at Cincinnati, Ohio, April 6th and 7th 1881.* Cincinnati: The Society, 1885.

———. *Report of the Proceedings of the Eighteenth Meeting of the Society of the Army of the Tennessee.* Cincinnati: The Society, 1893.

White, Ronald C. *American Ulysses: A Life of Ulysses S. Grant.* New York: Random House, 2017.

Williams, Geo. W. *A History of the Negro Troops in the War of the Rebellion, 1861–1865.* New York: Harper's, 1888.

Wilson, Keith P., and Keith Malcolm Wilson. *Campfires of Freedom: The Camp Life of Black Soldiers During the Civil War*. Kent, OH: Kent State University Press, 2002.

Woodworth, Steven E., Charles D. Grear, et al. *The Vicksburg Campaign, March 29–May 18, 1863*. Carbondale: Southern Illinois University Press, 2013.

## Online Resources

"1860s: Advanced Civil War Weapons." *Stolen History Blog*, Dec 6, 2020. https://www.stolenhistory. org/articles/1860s-advanced-civil-war-weapons.169/. Accessed July 24, 2021.

Drake, Rebecca Blackwell. "Union Headquarters: The Lum House: Recollections of Vicksburg from The Personal Memoirs of Julia Dent Grant." Battle of Raymond website, http://battleofraymond. org/history/lum.htm. Accessed Sept. 12, 2021.

Blake, Kellee. "'First in the Path of the Firemen'; The Fate of the 1890 Population Census, Part 2." *Prologue Magazine* 28, no. 1 (spring 1996). https://www.archives.gov/publications/prologue/1996/ spring/1890-census-2.html. Accessed Nov. 4, 2021.

"Grant, Frederick D." Wisconsin Veterans' Museum. https://wisvetsmuseum.pastperfectonline.com/ byperson?keyword=Grant%2C+Frederick+D. Accessed Oct. 1, 2021.

"Multi-Firing Weapons of the Civil War." The Collector's Firearms Blog, April 29, 2021. https:// www.collectorsfirearms.com/blog/post/multi-firing-guns-of-the-civil-war.html. Accessed July 24, 2021.

"Nux vomica." APA Dictionary of Psychology. https://dictionary.apa.org/nux-vomica. Accessed March 28, 2022.

"'Old Shady': Civil War Vet Who Died in GF was Cook for Gen. Sherman." *Grand Forks Herald*, April 28, 2011. Online at https://www.grandforksherald.com/2153610-old-shady-civil-war-vet-who-died-gf-was-cook-gen-sherman. Accessed Aug. 28, 2021.

"Stephen T. Gordon." Brass Net. https://www.brasshistory.net/Gordon%20History.pdf. Accessed Oct. 24, 2021.

"Strychnos nux-vomica L." United States Department of Agriculture, Natural Resources Conservation Service. https://plants.sc.egov.usda.gov/home/plantProfile?symbol=STNU4. Accessed March 28, 2022.

Ulysses S. Grant National Historic Site. "Frederick Dent Grant Joins His Father on the Battlefield." https://www.nps.gov/articles/000/frederick-dent-grant-joins-his-father-on-the-battlefield.htm. Accessed Oct. 8, 2021.

Ulysses S. Grant Presidential Library. Ulysses S. Grant Genealogy. https://www.usgrantlibrary.org/ usgrant/genealogy.

Ural, Susannah J. "Favorite Sons of the Civil War." History Net, undated, republished from *America's Civil War*, March 2014. https://www.historynet.com/favorite-sons-civil-war.htm. Accessed August 21, 2021.

Warren, Andrea. "Young Frederick Grant Goes to War." Nonfiction Minute, November 16, 2017. https://www.nonfictionminute.org/the-nonfiction-minute/young-frederick-grant-goes-to-war. Accessed July 2, 2021.

For Younger Readers

Monjo, F. N. *The Vicksburg Veteran.* New York: Simon and Schuster, 1971. A fictionalized account of Fred's adventures for younger readers.

Warren, Andrea. *Under Siege!: Three Children at the Civil War Battle for Vicksburg.* New York: Melanie Kroupa Books/Farrar Straus Giroux, 2009. Although Warren confuses the term "casualties" with "dead," this is a reasonably accurate overview of the campaign for younger readers, interweaving the experiences of Fred Grant with those of two local children, 10-year-old Lucy McRae, daughter of a prosperous local businessman, who had two brothers in gray, and 11-year-old William "Willie" Wilberforce Lord Jr., son of an Episcopal minister.

# INDEX

*Acknowledgments*

While writing is generally a rather solitary activity, there are often many people who contribute to the process in various ways.

Professors Jeremy Black, Dave Powell, David Madden, Chris Mackowski, and Jonathan Beard were kind enough to read the manuscript, offering valuable suggestions.

I received useful advice on particular questions from John A. Braden, great-great grandson of John Braden of the 5th Michigan; David Nelson, who had a great-grandfather in the 13th New York Militia and the U.S. Navy; Linda Robinson, of The Squadron A Association, who tracked down George H. Barnes; and Professor John Boardman, who had some kinfolk in the 1st Minnesota, for some useful, and amusing, information about horses.

Prof. David S. Nolen, Associate Editor/Reference Librarian, Ulysses S. Grant Presidential Library/Congressional and Political Research Center, Mitchell Memorial Library, Mississippi State University; A. J. Muhammad, of the Jean Blackwell Hutson Research and Reference Division, Schomburg Center for Research in Black Culture, New York Public Library; David Mindel, of the Murphy Library Special Collections/ARC, University of Wisconsin-La Crosse; and Nick Sacco and Amber Dumler, of the National Park Service, were very helpful in response to inquiries.

As always, the good people at the Schwarzman Building of the New York Public Library, and particularly those of the Milstein Division of United States History, were immensely helpful.

Last, but by no means least, thanks are in order to Ted Savas, and his staff at Savas Beatie, particularly Sarah Keeney, David J. Snyder, Veronica Kane, and Ryan Quint for bringing this book into print.

— A. A. Nofi

BATTLES & LEADERS SERIES

# THE BATTLE
## OF
# JACKSON,
## MISSISSIPPI

MAY 14, 1863

Chris Mackowski

Exclusive Excerpt

SB

Savas Beatie
California

# TABLE of CONTENTS

# FOREWORD

by Terrence J. Winschel

"VICKSBURG IS the key," declared President Abraham Lincoln and asserted that "the war can never be brought to a close until that key is in our pocket." This powerful statement was no exaggeration as Confederate cannon mounted on the bluffs overlooking the Mississippi River at Vicksburg denied that important avenue of commerce to Northern shipping. It was imperative for the administration in Washington to open the river to enable the rich agricultural bounty of the land, especially that of the "Old Northwest," to reach world markets. Pocketing that key would give the North unfettered control of the Mississippi River. It would also divide the South in two, sever major Confederate supply and communications lines, achieve a major objective of the Anaconda Plan, and effectively seal the doom of Richmond. Thus, Vicksburg was a city of unparalleled significance, and the "Gibraltar of the Confederacy" would prove a tough nut to crack.

Throughout 1862 and into 1863 Union land and naval forces made several attempts to capture the city to no avail. Finally, after months of frustration and failure, in the spring of 1863 combined land and naval forces led by Maj. Gen. Ulysses S. Grant and R. Adm. David Dixon Porter launched a campaign that resulted in the fall of Vicksburg on July 4, 1863. Although Grant would later admit that he could not have taken Vicksburg without the navy's assistance, his land operations have been termed "The most brilliant campaign ever waged on American soil." As such, it warrants detailed examination by professional soldiers and students of military history.

Many excellent histories have been written about the campaign at large and even specific aspects of Grant's operations. The battle of Jackson, fought on May 14, 1863, was a key action during the Vicksburg campaign as it resulted in the capture of Mississippi's capital city. More importantly, Union victory scattered Confederate forces under Gen. Joseph E. Johnston to the winds, which provided Grant's force security as he wheeled his Army of the Tennessee west toward its ultimate objective, Vicksburg. It also firmly established Grant's army as a wedge between Lt. Gen. John C. Pemberton's army in Vicksburg and those forces of Johnston that would reoccupy Jackson and pose a threat to Grant's rear throughout the long 47-day siege of the fortress city on the Mississippi River. Grant's position prevented effective communications between the two Confederate generals, keeping them from acting in concert with one another to raise the siege and rescue the beleaguered garrison.

In light of these results, it is hard to understand why most works on the Vicksburg campaign devote but few pages to the battle of Jackson. The lengthiest and most detailed work to date is *The Battle of Jackson May 14, 1863/The Siege of Jackson July 10-17, 1863* (158 pages) by Edwin C. Bearss and Warren Grabau, released by Gateway Press in 1981. This volume is now hard to find and treasured by those who have it. Ed Bearss also included a chapter on the battle of Jackson in Volume II of his trilogy *The Vicksburg Campaign,* recently reprinted by Savas Beatie.

Chris Mackowski, the editor of the *Emerging Civil War* blog, and book series by the same name published by

Savas Beatie, corrects that oversight and fills a significant void in the literature on the campaign with this volume. Mackowski, author or co-author of more than 15 books, focuses his talented pen and marvelous storytelling ability to detail the battle for control of Mississippi's capital city. He combines enough detail to satisfy the serious student of the war and color to appeal to the novice that makes for a smooth-flowing and easy-to-read narrative that is a welcomed addition to the fast-growing field of literature on the Vicksburg campaign.

Terrence J. Winschel
Historian (ret.) Vicksburg National Military Park
Author of the two-volume *Triumph & Defeat:*
*The Vicksburg Campaign*

# INTRODUCTION

IN MAY 2018, the American Battlefield Trust (ABT) invited me to visit Mississippi as co-host of a series of Facebook Live videos to commemorate the 155th anniversary of Grant's Vicksburg campaign. I would be traveling with my partner in crime and frequent collaborator, Kris White, the Trust's senior education manager, and Conner Townsend, the Trust's social media manager. Along the way, we'd be joined by Brig. Gen. (ret.) Parker Hills, Timothy B. Smith, Terry Winschel, and historians from the National Park Service as special guests to help share the stories of one of Grant's most impressive feats of the war.

I'm an Eastern Theater guy by background, experience, and proximity, so I had to do some studying up in order to hold my own among such a constellation of western talent. Winschel, retired chief historian of Vicksburg National Military Park, is a legend, and Tim Smith is among the Civil War historians whose work I most admire. I was unfamiliar with Gen. Hills but soon came to appreciate his incredible encyclopedic memory and passion for the story (and I'm lucky that we've since become friends).

I knew in advance I had to pick my battles, so to speak. The Vicksburg campaign was vast, stretching from the city's July 4, 1863, surrender all the way back into the early summer of '62. For our ABT trip, we were focusing

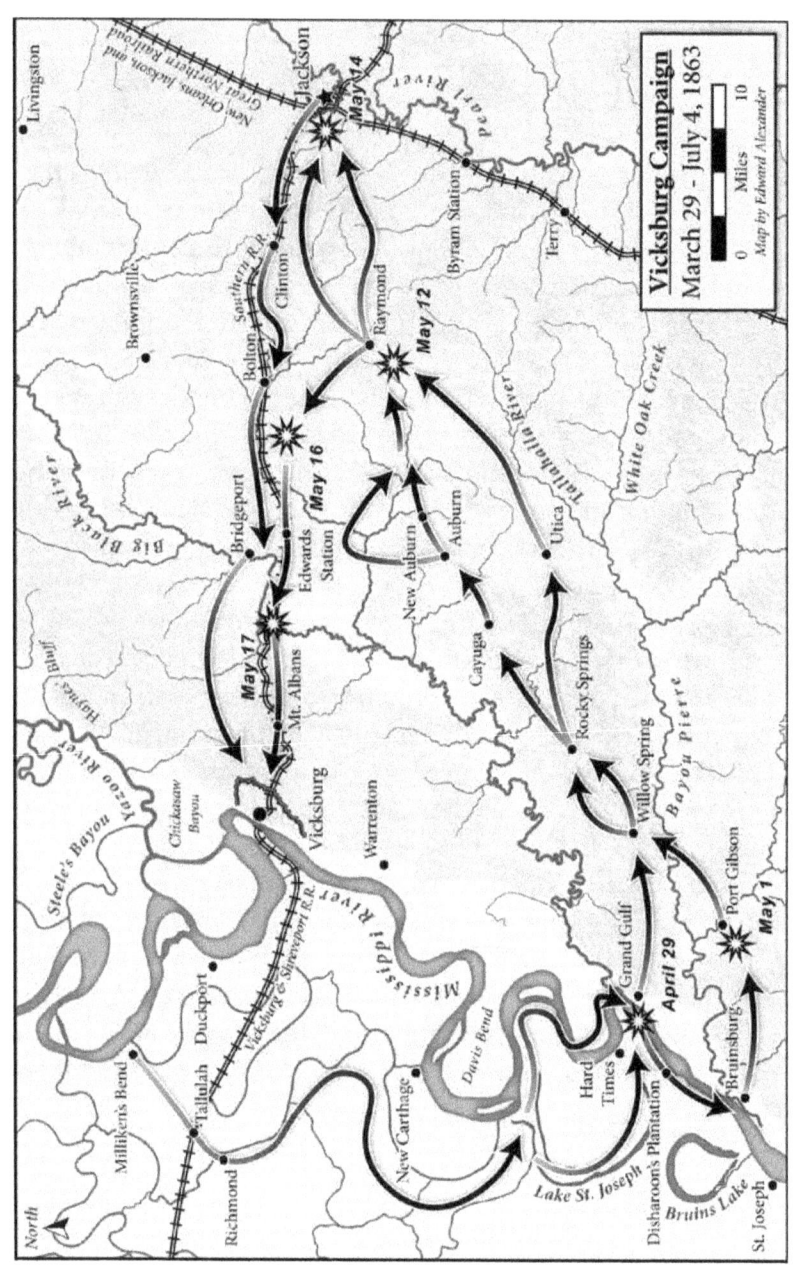

Vicksburg Campaign
March 29 - July 4, 1863
Map by Edward Alexander

VICKSBURG CAMPAIGN

Some historians have called Grant's overland campaign through Mississippi "the Blitzkrieg of the Civil War." Grant's May 14 capture of Jackson—on the heels of an unimpeded river crossing and successes at Port Gibson, Grand Gulf, and Raymond—set the stage for his pivot west to finally invest Vicksburg by land. Victories at Champion Hill and the Big Black River would bolster Federal confidence prior to assaults on May 19 and 22 and, finally, a 47-day siege. It would also give Grant important insights he would put into play during his 1864 Overland Campaign in Virginia.

*Edward Alexander*

on only the overland actions leading to the gates of the city, as well as the siege itself. If we mark time beginning with the river crossing on April 30, that still manages to encompass 67 days of action, including battles on May 1, 12, 14, 16, 17, 19, and 22, with lots of smaller actions and anecdotes sprinkled in until the surrender of the city on July 4, now famously known as "the most glorious fourth."

For context, let me remind you that I'm a "Stonewall" Jackson fanboy, so the vast majority of my knowledge of events on May 2, 1863, and the eight days that follow are focused on the battle of Chancellorsville, Jackson's accidental wounding by his own men that day, the conclusion of Robert E. Lee's so-called "greatest victory," and Jackson's death on May 10. In that regard, Grant's crossing of the Mississippi could not have been better timed. Like me, most of Richmond's attention was focused on, and absorbed by, events along the Rappahannock, not along the Mississippi. While Jefferson Davis was himself a Mississippian—a resident of Warren County, of which Vicksburg is the county seat—poor health had him laid low by late April, so he struggled to find the energy to deal with the faraway events in his home state when closer events loomed with so much more pressing immediacy.

I set about familiarizing myself as much as possible with the events of those 67 days, padding what I learned with as much additional context as I could. Aside from this breadth, I also wanted to pick something I could go deep on. Aside from their general expertise, I knew Parker would have Raymond covered because he'd personally done so much to preserve that battlefield; I knew Tim would have Champion Hill covered because he wrote "the" book on the battle (and was working on his five-volume magnus opus on the campaign, which has been fantastic); I knew Terry and the NPS folks would have Vicksburg itself covered because of the national military park.

In this context, I chose to become the "instant expert" on the battle of Jackson, although not because of any process of elimination. I chose the battle because my oldest son is named Jackson, christened by his older sister after Stonewall. But even Stonewall Jackson didn't play into my decision, despite my appreciation of him. I did it simply because the battle and my oldest son shared a name.

As I researched the battle of Jackson, news of the fall of the city was almost always preceded, surrounded, and drowned out by news of the fall of the general. This was true in newspapers, diary accounts, and even postwar memoirs. A Google search of "Jackson" in May 1863 (if we can imagine such a thing!) would have certainly returned hundreds if not thousands of lamentations about Stonewall compared to perhaps dozens of mentions of the Mississippi capital. (For kicks, try it yourself: "Jackson + May 1863"). Earl Van Dorn's death at the hands of a jealous husband might make a cameo appearance in the search, too, because he was the one-time commander of the Vicksburg garrison—"Mississippi" might have tripped an algorithm somewhere.

The ABT trip to Mississippi became one of the real highlights of my Civil War career, and my meager attempt to be the crew's expert on the battle of Jackson went smoothly. Kris chuckled at me because, of the two of us, he's usually the one who descends to the microtactical level and I'm usually the big-picture "story" guy, so it amused him to see me go into the weeds.

After the trip, I thought, *I should really do something with all this Jackson research I've done.* I didn't know what, exactly, but I figured I'd get around to writing something at some point. The sheaf of notes, scribbled across pages and pages of yellow ruled paper, sat on a pile on the catch-all top of a filing cabinet next to my desk.

For years.

In 2021, as Emerging Civil War prepared to celebrate its tenth anniversary with a short commemorative series of books, we honed in on Vicksburg as the topic of one of the volumes. *Ah ha!* I thought. *Now's the chance to dust off that research on the battle of Jackson and use it to write an original piece for the Vicksburg volume.* I hadn't revisited the material since the trip, although it didn't take too long to freshen up.

The body of work on the battle of Jackson isn't expansive. Aside from an impossible-to-find short hardcover by Ed Bearss and Warren Grabau written in 1981, no stand-alone work on the battle seemed to exist. (Jim Woodrick, former Civil War historian for the state of Mississippi, has a great little book on the July 1863 siege of Jackson.) Where the battle of Jackson is covered in campaign histories, it typically gets no more than three pages, if that. Even Ed's book covers the battle in a volume that also includes the July siege and three other post-Vicksburg actions.

Here was another chance to go deep.

As my notes took shape in narrative form, that narrative grew and grew. I thought I'd write something hefty in the six-thousand-word range. Then eight thousand. Then suddenly a dozen. And by then, I knew I'd outgrown the ECW Vicksburg volume—and I wasn't even done yet.

What was I going to do with this thing?

During one of my regular conversations with Ted Savas, I mentioned this quandary to him. "Heyyyyy!" he replied. Ted has a way of drawing out the last "y" when he gets a flash of inspiration. "I have an idea. What if we do this. . . ."

And here *this* is.

It will likely take you longer to read about the battle of Jackson than it took the men to fight it. However, I wanted to provide the most comprehensive account to date of the action there. The May 14, 1863, battle does not rank as the most important of Grant's Mississippi campaign, but it does probably rank as the most overlooked. Port Gibson was the first; the fall of Grand Gulf might be the most strategically important; Raymond has had extensive preservation efforts bolstering its story; Champion Hill was easily the most consquential. Perhaps only the flash-in-the-pan fight at the Big Black gets less love than Jackson.

Here, then, is the story of the May 14, 1863, battle of Jackson, Mississippi—with thanks to Kris White and the American Battlefield Trust and inspired, at its very core, by my own son, Jackson.

I assure you, that's a lot of love.

# 1

## OLD JOE

JOSEPH E. Johnston was unfit for service and flat-out said so to his boss: "I shall go immediately, although unfit for field service."[1]

But go the general did, departing on May 10, 1863, from Tullahoma, Tennessee, for Jackson, Mississippi, on the peremptory orders of the Confederate Secretary of War, James Seddon. A Union army had made landfall on the east bank of the Mississippi River and was now operating somewhere in the state's interior. Control of the river was at stake. The populace—the white populace, anyway—was panicked. Confederate President Jefferson Davis expressed concern about his home state. Johnston had to go sort things out.

Johnston did not want to make the trip, though—had, in fact, resisted going to Mississippi for months. He had insisted that the Confederate army in middle Tennessee, also under his command, needed his direct supervision more than the army in Mississippi did. He had worried that the commander in Tennessee, Gen. Braxton Bragg, was distracted by the failing health of his dying wife. For good measure, Johnston had also complained that old

---

1 Johnston to Seddon, 9 May 1863, *The War of the Rebellion: A Compilation of the Official Records of the Union and Confederate Armies* (Washington, D.C.: Government Printing Office, 1889), Series 1. Vol. 23, Pt. 3, 826, hereafter abbreviated as "O.R."

GEN. JOSEPH E. JOHNSTON

One soldier of the Army of Tennessee described Joe Johnston thus: "Fancy, if you please, a man about fifty years old, rather small of stature but firmly built, an open countenance, and a keen, restless eye that seemed to read your inmost thoughts. In his dress he was a perfect dandy. He ever wore the finest clothes that could be obtained, carrying out in dress and the paraphernalia of the soldier the plan adopted by the War Department at Richmond, never omitting anything, even to the trappings of his horse, bridle and saddle. His head was decorated with a star and feather, his coat with every star and embellishment, and he wore a bright new sash, big gauntlets, and silver spurs. He was the very picture of a general."

*Library of Congress*

war injuries still ailed him, thus making him too unwell to serve in the field.

The thing Johnston worried about most, though, was his reputation. His litany of complaints served primarily as a smokescreen to defend it.

"[O]ld Joe was a yerker," said Pvt. Sam Watkins of the Army of Tennessee admiringly. "He took all the tricks. He was a commander."[2] Arthur Fremantle, a British colonel observing the American war in the spring and summer of 1863, was impressed by the "commander's" bearing:

> In appearance, General Joseph E. Johnston, commonly called Joe Johnston, is rather below the middle height, spare, soldierlike, and well set up; his features are good, and he has lately taken to wear a grayish beard. He is a Virginian by birth, and appears to be about fifty-[six] years old. He talks in a calm, deliberate, and confident manner; to me he was extremely affable, but he certainly possesses the power of keeping people at a distance when he chooses and his officers evidently stand in great awe of him.[3]

As a career officer, Johnston had an impressive resume that he'd begun building during the war with Mexico decades earlier. After, he served with distinction in the antebellum army and, when civil war broke out, became the highest-ranking officer to defect to the Confederacy. A disagreement over how to count that pre-war service when it came time to issue ranks in the Confederate army led to a dispute between Johnston and President Davis: Johnston fell behind Samuel Cooper, Albert Sidney Johnston, and Robert E. Lee on the list of seniority but

---

2 Sam Watkins, *Co. Aytch: A Side Show of the Big Show*, 2nd ed. (Chattanooga, TN: Times Printing Company, 1900), 106.

3 Arthur Fremantle, *Three Months in the Southern States* (London: William Blackwood and Sons, 1863), 116.

CONFEDERATE PRESIDENT
JEFFERSON DAVIS

A native of Mississippi, Jefferson Davis owned
a plantation on the outskirts of Vicksburg—as
did his brother, Joseph—so the military situation
along the river was not only of vital national
importance to him but also of keen personal
interest.

*Library of Congress*

thought he should rank higher. His placement in the
number-four slot "seeks to tarnish my fair fame as a
soldier and a man, earned by more than thirty years of

laborious and perilous service," he complained.[4] Slighted, the too-proud Johnston held a grudge against Davis that ever thereafter poisoned their relationship. "His hatred of Jeff Davis amounts to a religion," diarist Mary Chesnut would write of the embittered Virginian. "With him it colors all things."[5] Indeed, says scholar Stephen Cushman with the benefit of a century and a half of hindsight, "The two men did not trust, cooperate with, or forgive each other as long as they lived."[6]

Nonetheless Johnston was one of the Confederacy's true war heroes after earning victory at First Manassas in July 1861 (though, in fact, he had little to do with it). He remained in command of Confederate forces in his native Virginia through May 31, 1862, when a shell fragment knocked him out of action at the battle of Seven Pines. This was the war wound he would thereafter milk whenever called on to perform a task he didn't want to do.

Davis had disapproved of Johnston's strategy during the spring campaign on the Virginia Peninsula and, in fact, Johnston's wounding must've seemed at least a partial relief to the Confederate commander in chief. Robert E. Lee's subsequent success as Johnston's replacement made the switch permanent. As much as Johnston wanted his old army back, Davis had no intention of replacing Lee, even after Johnston had recuperated. Rechristened the Army of Northern Virginia, it was Lee's army in spirit as well as in fact, and "Old Joe" would ever after be on the outs.

---

4   Johnston to Davis, 12 September 1861, O.R., series IV, Vol. I, 607.

5   Mary Boykin Chestnut, *A Diary from Dixie*, Isabella Martin and Myrta Lockett Avary, eds. (New York: D. Appleton and Company, 1905), 248-49.

6   Stephen Cushman, "Joseph E. Johnston," *Essential Civil War Curriculum*, https://www.essentialcivilwarcurriculum.com/joseph-e.-johnston.html (accessed 10 January 2021).

To solve the problem, Davis promoted Johnston to command of the Western Theater—from the Appalachian Mountains to the Mississippi River. A position of high stakes required a skilled commander, and like many others, Davis respected Johnston's reputation even if he did not like the man or approve of his spring performance on the Peninsula. Of the tools available, Johnston seemed best equipped to handle the vast responsibility in the West. "Whatever man can do will be done by him," Davis would tell Mississippi lawmakers, expressing "perfect confidence."[7]

Johnston, for his part—with bruises to his ego to nurse—believed Davis promoted him as an elaborate ruse to set him up for failure. "[T]he forces . . . under my command are greatly inferior in number to those of the enemy opposed to them," he wrote, sounding much like his old nemesis, Union Maj. Gen. George McClellan, who habitually overestimated enemy strength.[8] Worse, in Johnston's opinion, the geographic expanse under his charge was too vast to cover with the troops available to him. He sought on several occasions to consolidate the two main armies in the theater, Bragg's Army of Tennessee and Lt. Gen. John Pemberton's Army of Vicksburg. Davis refused, instead ordering Johnston to establish a headquarters that "in his judgment will best secure facilities for ready communication with the troops within the limits of his

7   Jefferson Davis, speech to Mississippi legislature, 26 December 1862. From Rice University's online Papers of Jefferson Davis. https:// jeffersondavis.rice.edu/archives/documents/jefferson-davis-speech-jackson-miss-0 (accessed 3 March 2021). Text from *The Papers of Jefferson Davis*, Volume 8, 565-84, transcribed from the 29 December 1862 edition of the Memphis *Appeal*, which, according to *The Papers*, was being published in Jackson at that time.

8   Joseph E. Johnston, *Narrative of Military Operations, Directed, During the Late War Between the States, by Joseph E. Johnston* (New York: D. Appleton and Company, 1874), 149.

command. . . ." Wherever headquarters turned out to be, Johnston's orders explicitly stated that he should not feel tethered to the spot but rather "repair in person to any part of said command whenever his presence may for the time be necessary or desirable."[9]

From Davis's perspective, Richmond was too far from both Tennessee and Mississippi, and "he thought it necessary to have an officer nearer, with authority to transfer troops from one army to another in an emergency," as Johnston later explained. "If such an officer was needed," he continued, "I certainly was not the proper selection; for I had already expressed the opinion that such transfers were impracticable, because each of the two armies was greatly inferior to its antagonist; and they were too far from each other for such mutual dependence."[10]

Johnston thus set up shop in central Tennessee and thereafter did his best to pretend the Vicksburg army wasn't really his concern. "The only effect . . . of my taking direction of affairs," he wrote a political ally, "would be my being responsible for Pemberton's generalship, instead of himself. If he entitled himself to praise, robbing him of it. If he deserves blame, bearing it for him."[11]

Whenever Richmond pressed him, Johnston responded with his smokescreen of concerns, complaints, and ailments. By early April, when Bragg's wife's health recovered and Johnston no longer had that distraction as an excuse, he "afterward became sick" himself and, as he reported to Jefferson Davis on April 10, "am not

9   Special Orders 275, 24 November 1862, O.R. XVII, 758.

10  Johnston, *Narrative*, 154-55.

11  Joseph Johnston to Louis Wigfall, 8 March 1863, quoted in John R. Lundberg, "I Am Too Late," *The Vicksburg Campaign, March 29-May 18, 1863*, Steven E. Woodworth and Charles D. Grear, eds. (Carbondale, IL: Southern Illinois University Press, 2013), 119.

now able to serve in the field."[12] Sympathetic biographer Craig L. Symonds describes Johnston as "suffering from incompletely healed wounds, exacerbated now by his frequent travels," adding apologetically that Johnston exercised only "nominal command."[13] Historian John Lundberg counters that "Johnston used his discomfort as a cover for not pursuing his command in Mississippi more proactively."[14]

But on May 10, 1863, with a Federal army under Maj. Gen. Ulysses S. Grant driving boldly through Mississippi's interior, Johnston had no choice but to go west.

## End of Excerpt

---

12  Johnston to Davis, 10 April 1863, O.R. XXII, Pt. 2, 745.

13  Craig L. Symonds, *Joseph E. Johnston: A Civil War Biography* (New York: W.W. Norton & Co., 1992), 201.

14  Lundberg, 120.

About the Editor

Albert A. Nofi has a doctorate in military history from the City University of New York and is the author or editor of more than 40 books. He is a founding member and director of the New York Military Affairs Symposium and a regular contributor to StrategyPage.com. The sometimes sea cook lives in Brooklyn.